WAGNER
A case history

WAGNER
A case history

MARTIN VAN AMERONGEN

Translated by
Stewart Spencer and Dominic Cakebread

J.M. Dent & Sons Ltd
London Melbourne

First published in Great Britain 1983 by J.M. Dent & Sons Ltd
English translation copyright © 1983 Stewart Spencer and
Dominic Cakebread

Originally published in Dutch, copyright © 1983 by
Uitgeverij De Arbeiderspers, Amsterdam, under the title
De buikspreker van God

Phototypeset in 11/13½ Linotron Plantin by
Tradespools Ltd, Frome
Printed and made in Great Britain by
Biddles Ltd, Guildford
for J.M. Dent & Sons Ltd
Aldine House, 33 Welbeck Street, London W1M 8LX

British Library Cataloguing in Publication Data

Amerongen, Martin van
   Wagner.
   1. Wagner, Richard
   2. Composers—Germany—Biography
   I. Title   II. Spencer, Stewart
   III. Cakebread, Dominic
   782.1'092'4   782.1'092'4

ISBN 0–460–04618–7

Contents

1

Bayreuth in peace-time

From Karl Marxstrasse you come directly to Nibelungen-strasse. You continue straight on past Meistersingerstrasse, Parsifalstrasse and Rheingoldstrasse. You go on past the Holländer Rooms, then turn right, and find yourself in Siegfried Wagner-Allee, which takes you up towards the top of the Green Hill, where you will find Richard Wagner's Festspielhaus. You can also get there from the station by turning off to the right along Bürgerreuther Strasse, which used to be known as Adolf Hitlerstrasse, but we are not concerned with that now.

Dr Oswald Georg Bauer, the head of the press office of the Bayreuth Festival, allows me a brief glimpse of the interior of the building. We go down towards the famous 'mystical abyss', the sunken, half-covered orchestra pit in which both orchestra and conductor are completely hidden from the audience's view. I would certainly like to have gone and stood on the conductor's podium, where Hans Richter, Karl Böhm and Pierre Boulez had all stood as Valhalla went up in flames. Everywhere else in the building the occupants avoid fire as the devil avoids holy water. 'That's because everything here is made of wood – the auditorium, the floor and the seating. Hence the famous acoustics,' says Bauer. 'There are three firemen in permanent attendance through-out each of the performances, so we hope they get at least some enjoyment out of being here, otherwise six hours of *Götterdämmerung* must seem like a very long time.'

The auditorium is constructed in the form of a classical amphitheatre: a semicircle without the usual side balconies that would enable you to wave at your friends in the stalls. In addition to Wagner's other dislikes, what he hated most of all were traditional opera audiences who went to the theatre largely in order to be seen. As a punishment he designed the most advanced and the least comfortable theatre of his day. Our guide taps on the floorboards with the heel of his shoe. 'This floor is the original one from 1876, the year the *Ring* was first produced here. The wood had previously been used for a sort of raft and was already about 120 years old when it was installed here. The floor, too, is regarded as irreplaceable. You could think of it as a Stradivarius. You couldn't replace the sound-board without the instrument's being irreparably damaged.'

The 57,000 tickets at the Festival's disposal are generally sold out at least a year in advance. The computer churns out an average of 220,000 copies of the standard letter, beginning, 'We regret to inform you'.

Outside the sun is shining. The local cemetery lies a short distance from the centre of the town. All the graves, without a single exception, look fresh and well cared-for. This is thanks to the small army of middle-aged women who, at the precise moment of my gazing at Liszt's mausoleum, all come pouring out across the cemetery, with a shopping bag in their left hand, and a little green watering-can in their right. Each grave is generously watered, without any distinction being made on grounds of status, class, colour or political conviction.

Close behind Liszt, Wagner's father-in-law, lie the mortal remains of Houston Stewart Chamberlain, Wagner's son-in-law and a kindred spirit as racial theorist. Half a row further on is the last resting place of Daniela Thode-von Bülow, one of the daughters from Cosima Wagner's first marriage to the conductor Hans von Bülow. Winifred Wagner shares a

2

tomb with her husband, Siegfried Wagner, and her eldest son, Wieland. Siegfried was in charge of the Bayreuth Festival in the years before and after the First World War, at a time when the German Nationalists dominated the Green Hill. Winifred's period of artistic control coincided for the most part with the Third Reich, which did nothing at all for the composer's reputation. After the Second World War, it was on Wieland and his brother Wolfgang that the difficult task fell of scraping away all the brown deposit which had become encrusted in the course of the decades.

Gondrom's bookshop in Maximilianstrasse has in stock five shelves full of Wagneriana and a few inches of anti-Wagneriana. I leaf through a few pages of a little book entitled *Bayreuth for Beginners*, an outrageously irreverent work from the pen of one Herbert Rosendorfer. He calls Wagner's *Die Meistersinger von Nürnberg* 'a mammoth operetta' and speaks nostalgically of the sensuous way in which he once heard Siegfried's Funeral March played at an accordion competition at Unna in Westphalia. This particular edition of the book is dated 1969, when the author still used the name Vibber Tøgesen, since–as he says in his foreword–the name Rosendorfer would undoubtedly have struck Wagnerians as sounding too Jewish. That was why he had temporarily given himself such impeccable Aryan credentials: 'he is a descendent of Smørre Sigjav, the legendary creator of the Sigjav-Thing near Lake Fämund in Norway'.

One shelf further down, Leo Fremgen (*Richard Wagner heute* ['Richard Wagner today'], 1977) analyses the deeper lying reasons for anti-Wagnerianism today and in the past. 'What we see in the case of Wagner's enemies,' he says, 'is nothing but pure prejudice or innate hostility.' Innate hostility? By that the writer can be thinking only of the

3

crafty Jews, who gave the Master himself so much to think about. The reader is set at rest: Wagner is 'ineradicable' ('unausrottbar'). It looks as though terms are still being used in the composer's defence which one would think had disappeared from the language with the downfall of the Third Reich.

The gardens at the back of Wahnfried, the former headquarters of the enterprise, have not changed in the slightest since the days when the young Wolfgang and Wieland used to jump around on the lawn with their sisters Verena and Friedelind, brandishing their tiny spears and dressed up as miniature versions of Wotan, Fricka, Freia and Siegfried. The house has been open to the public for a number of years. The dome-shaped reception room, where Wagner once held court, is now used for recorded concerts. Five tourists, with cameras dangling in front of them, are listening to a recording of the Siegfried Idyll, broadcast over two loudspeakers.

In the next room is a collection of curios, intended to show that Wahnfried is not at all blind to the more trivial aspects of Wagner's life and works. The relics on show here include the Master's teeth and Cosima's bottle of smelling-salts. It appears that a few years ago the advertising section of the weekly magazine *Der Spiegel* tried to sell an annual subscription to Herr Richard Wagner, D-8580 Bayreuth. The artists' café Sammet-Angermann once used to serve Lohengrin trout, Siegfried schnitzels and Wotan ham à la Valhalla.

A polemical rhyme written in 1881 satirizes the incestuous goings-on in the first act of *Die Walküre*:

> Here is Siegmund and his twin-sister.
> They'd scarcely met before he kissed her.
> Now they're into heavy petting,
> And all the time we risk forgetting

How unspeakably disgusting
Is the love for which they're lusting,
Driving Sieglind' and her brother
Into sleeping with each other.

The opposition which Wagner used to evoke is systematically catalogued in a volume published in 1876 under the title *Dictionary of Insults, containing terms of abuse, derision, hostility and slander which have been used against the Master Richard Wagner, his works and his supporters by his enemies and detractors*. No, Wagner has never been uncontroversial, this executioner of modern art, this cultural vandal, this mad fool, this Don Quixote, this *fou d'orgueil*, this scourge of God, this great Jew-eater, this arrogant Jew-boy, this Royal Bavarian boot-licker, this Marat of music, H.R.H. Richard I of Madcap Villa, Valhalla Weiha Lawei Wagner.

In spite of everything, he lived to be seventy. He lies buried in the same grave as his wife, in the garden at the rear of the house. The huge, anonymous, marble slab is symmetrical and overgrown with ivy. An American, with a green Michelin guide in his back pocket, gazes at the monument in reverential silence.

'Do you know,' I say severely, 'that in 1945 your fellow countrymen danced the jitterbug on this grave, wearing bearskins from the theatre wardrobe?'

'Really?' the man asks. He seems shocked. But then he pulls himself together: 'Well, I'm not surprised.'

2

A skyscraper full of Wagneriana

After Jesus Christ and Napoleon, Wagner is one of the most written about figures in history. Yet the fact remains that, according to the literary historian Hans Mayer, 'The first step towards a scholarly interpretation of Wagner's intellectual and artistic development is still barely visible'.

The off-hand way in which Wagner sought to ensure a place for himself in cultural history has resulted in Wagner scholars having spent the whole of the last century and a half locked in a struggle between polemicism, on the one hand, and canonization, on the other. A whole skyscraper could be filled just with the writers who have concerned themselves with his canonization. Even today one can still see signs of the over-zealous manner in which Wahnfried has touched up the human, all too human features of the composer's portrait.

This is true, for a start, of the Master's autobiography *Mein Leben*, a work as amusing as it is unreliable, and described by Friedrich Nietzsche as a 'fable convenue'. Certainly, circumstances were less than ideal for an objective record of events. The Master dictated and Frau Cosima wrote everything down, using the gold pen which his former mistress, Mathilde Wesendonck, had once given him, and this of course required a certain tact in Wagner's account of the facts.

Cosima, for her part, constantly carried around with her a red pencil, especially when Wagner studies began to grow more intensive after the death of the composer. Whenever she came across the expression 'after the revolution' in one of her late husband's letters, she would alter the wording to read 'later'. And if she stumbled upon one of his frivolous little verses, like the one which ran 'The Sabbatical Christian does ever so well: whenever he pisses, there's never a smell', it was removed from Wagner's unpublished papers. Wagner derived a great deal of pleasure from his amorous conquests and in one of his letters he included a colourful description of the way in which the then Cosima von Bülow, in the early days of their young love, had sunk down on her knees before him and covered his hands with kisses—this passage was naturally struck out from the correspondence at the time it was being prepared for publication. Indeed, the letters which passed between Wagner and his second wife were virtually all destroyed by Cosima herself. The two of them discussed the desirability of such a step on 13 June 1881, two years before Wagner's death. It was not that they had anything to hide from the outside world. On the contrary, their reason for doing so was that they were afraid of dying before their son Siegfried ('Fidi') was sufficiently mature to be able to read the correspondence without his soul being irreparably damaged. In the event, 'Fidi' did not even trouble to read his mother's Diaries, which she had dedicated to him, in spite of the fact that he had already reached the undeniably mature age of sixty when his mother died in 1930.

Cosima Wagner, who for years was the undisputed head of the Centre for the Falsification of Wagner's Memory, had a capable aide-de-camp in the person of Elisabeth Nietzsche, the philosopher's sister. The fact that Wagner and Nietzsche ended up at each other's throats did not for a moment prevent the two women from enjoying a warm friendship. 'Throughout the whole of this unhappy time,' wrote Cosima's biographer, Richard Graf Du Moulin

Eckart, 'Frau Cosima remained in close and constant contact with the philosopher's noble sister.' Much to her delight, Elisabeth Nietzsche was invited by Cosima to address her with 'the sisterly *du*' ('thou'): 'Do you know that Mrs Wagner and I say "du" and "Cosima" and "Elisabeth" to each other? It quite takes my breath away and I can scarcely bring myself to speak it.'

It must have been quite a spectacle, the sight of the two women sitting round the hearth and discussing in sisterly fashion how they could most effectively gloss over the pictures of the composer and the philosopher. In this way, Wagner's zeal on the barricades in revolutionary Dresden was trivialized to the level of an artistic whim inspired by youthful excess. And, for his part, Nietzsche was made to subscribe to the fateful theory of the *Übermensch*, or Superman. It would ultimately make both men more or less exploitable by the cultural politics of National Socialism. Never become an outstanding figure in the world of art or culture, unless you firmly intend taking your entire family with you to the grave.

Fifty years were to elapse after Wagner's death before the appearance of the first, uncoloured life of Wagner that could be taken seriously. This was Ernest Newman's four-volume *The Life of Richard Wagner*. The number of more or less sensible studies of Wagner to have followed has grown to fill at least a quarter of a shelf, while the skyscraper full of inflammatory rubbish still remains facing it, on the opposite side of the street. Secondary literature in which both the positive and the negative aspects of the composer are soberly balanced against each other still has something of a rarity value about it.

For, even today Wagner scholars, in spite of all their claims to objectivity, all too easily end up shouting at each other. Robert Gutman draws attention to an incident which took place in London in 1855 at the time of Wagner's conducting engagements there: 'In order to show contempt for Mendelssohn's "Italian" Symphony, he conducted it in kid gloves.' Martin Gregor-Dellin leaps to Wagner's defence: 'Did he put on kid gloves especially for this work?' Well, no. 'It was rather that he did not take them *off*.' Robert Gutman makes fun of Wagner's addiction to velvet neckerchiefs and silk underwear and in this context draws attention to a pink satin robe, designed by the composer himself, which included a sash five yards long. 'Considering his height of little over five feet, one must wonder how he managed to walk in these costumes without tripping.' But Martin Gregor-Dellin was able to lay his hands on Wagner's Swiss passport, which constituted his identification papers at the time of his political exile. A height of 5' 5½" is noted here, which means that the composer must have been 1.665 metres tall (one foot = 30 centimetres; and 5 inches = 15 centimetres). The conclusion of all this is that 'By contemporary standards, Wagner was by no means excessively small'.

It is incorrect, says Martin Gregor-Dellin, to name *Parsifal* in the same breath as Arthur Gobineau's book on racial theory, *Essai sur l'inégalité des races humaines*, since Wagner did not get to know the author and his principal work until well after the completion of his own *Bühnenweihfestspiel* ('Sacred stage festival play'). True enough, says Robert Gutman, but Wagner had absolutely no *need* of Gobineau's racist theories, since he himself had long been an expert in this field. This same *Parsifal* which, according to Martin Gregor-Dellin, was 'the work he cherished most' was, for all this, entrusted to the conductor Hermann Levi, the son of the High Rabbi of Giessen. 'True enough–but just one small point,' says Hartmut Zelinsky. 'Wagner had to entrust *Parsifal* to Levi, because Ludwig II had stressed that he would get the Munich Court Orchestra only if it included Levi, or else he would not get it at all.'

9

According to Curt von Westernhagen, Wagner's 'so-called anti-Semitism' has been much exaggerated. 'Wagner refused to sign "the mass petition against the growing influence of the Jews", which Dr Bernhard Förster, who was later to marry Elisabeth Nietzsche, had addressed to the Imperial Chancellor.' Perhaps I, too, might be allowed to join in the discussion for a moment. *Why* did Wagner – and only a fool would deny that he was the most inveterate anti-Semite – not sign this petition? The answer is to be found in his wife's Diaries: he refused to become involved because he was of the opinion that (a) he had already done his bit; (b) he had no desire to appeal directly to the Imperial Chancellor, Bismarck, whom he considered frivolous and capricious; and (c) he was of the opinion that, as far as the blockading of Germany's Judaization was concerned, the cause was already irretrievably lost (16 June 1880). The Diaries also show that a few weeks later, in the family circle at Wahnfried, Wagner explained his reasons in more detail. ' "And he expects me to sign *that!*" he cries out and reads us the absurdly pious terms in which the document has been formulated. He writes to Dr Förster, saying that ever since the events surrounding the petition against vivisection, he has resolved never again to have anything to do with such an initiative' (6 July 1880).

3

Daily life at the Villa Wahnfried

Cosima Wagner's Diaries, which were finally made public in 1976, provide an incomparably rich source of information not only about the inner life of the composer himself but also about that of his companion in life, Cosima. The latter, it is true, attempted to suppress a number of negative aspects about her husband after his death, but, within the cultural milieu of the nineteenth century, she was a woman of undeniable stature. Outwardly she looked like a hysterical leptosome, who must have fainted and burst into tears at least once every day. In practice, she was an extremely forceful woman, who knew exactly what she wanted and who realized that she had in her grasp one of the foremost geniuses of her time, a realization which allowed her to face every adversity, including the anger of her father, Franz Liszt, the despair of her first husband, Hans von Bülow, and the venomous gossip of public opinion.

She was not yet forty when, according to the French Wagnerian biographer Guy de Pourtalès, she became de facto general secretary of Wagner Enterprises. She soon had her hands full with her six children – two by Hans von Bülow, three by Wagner and, of course, Wagner himself. Wagner may have been 'the ventriloquist's puppet of God', as Nietzsche called the composer, but Cosima for her part was the ventriloquist's puppet of Wagner. In all the 2,500 pages of her Diaries I have found only one passage in which she gives any indication of having a mind of her own. This

11

was on 24 January 1869: 'Unfortunately R.'s passion for silk materials prompted me to make a remark which I would have done better to have left unsaid, since it led to a slight friction between us.' For the rest, the motto which 'Cosima Heferica Wagner' (as Richard called her) followed from morning till night was 'Dienen, dienen' ('To serve, to serve'). Was it advisable for her to read Schopenhauer, her husband's favourite philosopher? 'He advises me against it; a woman should come to philosophy through the man and the poet. Total agreement on my part' (2 January 1869).

Her love of Wagner must have been all-consuming. Thus the composer once found the following poem on his desk:

> Unsinning,
> Sublimely desiring,
> Grandly renouncing,
> Level-headed, persistent,
> Thoughtful, patient,
> Undaunted and loyal to your mission,
> Serenely inconstant,
> Solemnly impatient,
> Sublimely unlevel-headed,
> Fleeing delusion,
> Creatively destroying,
> Squanderously ordering,
> Prince of the people,
> Unconcerned with fame,
> Free from vanity,
> Frivolous,
> Fore-sighted,
> Innocent of suspicion!
> Kindly Gibichung,
> Wholly devoted,
> Deeply reserved,
> Immensely enthusiastic,
> Rousingly eloquent,
> Passionately silent,
> Hopelessly believing,

Merciless towards evil,
Champion of the weak,
Promulgator of truth,
Shying away from deceit,
Boldly unmasking,
Gently veiling,
Practitioner of love,
Exuding life,
World-stranger,
At home in nature's familiar realm,
Prophet of being,
Lord of appearance,
Controller of delusion.
Joy of the Will,
Bringer of redemption,
Blissfully creative,
All-sounding, beholding, competent,
Incomprehensible,
Innocent, free,
Child and God.

There is no doubt that Wagner felt much the same about Cosima. Whenever she was not to hand, he would prowl around his room like a caged polar bear. And when she returned, he would tell her in his typically plain-spoken way, 'But if you think I wrote a single bar without thinking of you and your Catholic eyes, may you be struck down by the curse of Hell'.

A few chosen members of the Wahnfried circle, including Richard Graf Du Moulin Eckart, had earlier been allowed a premature sight of Cosima's Diaries. Du Moulin Eckart called them a 'monument', since 'to a certain extent they embrace the whole intellectual and political world of the time'. Not to mention the preceding periods. The authors who were read within Wagner's family circle included Calderón, Goethe, Homer, Sophocles, Aeschylus, Wagner and Shakespeare. And when they were not reading, a good deal of weeping went on. 'Many tears this morning. God knows, they flow so freely that I cannot stop. But I try to hide them as best I can.'

The figure of the unhappy Hans von Bülow cast a permanent shadow over the idyll, at least during the early years of their life together. 'Thought a great, great deal about Hans.' When a letter arrived from a mutual acquaintance, announcing that the betrayed husband was so upset that he was thinking of unlearning German, it was not something which could be lightly passed over. On one occasion, Blandine, one of the daughters from Cosima's first marriage, improvised in her childish innocence a little tale about a naughty mother who left her loving husband in order to marry another man; it was very naughty of her and something which Blandine would never do. 'This in the presence of two servants, who immediately passed it on,' Cosima noted, wounded to the heart. 'I was forced to reprimand the child in a suitable way, thereby risking the loss of her love. God be my aid!'

The Diaries reflect in detail the cultivated milieu of two unmistakably literature-loving intellectuals. 'Sunday the 20th. R. wishes me good morning at 7 o'clock and says that he has been thinking a lot about Socrates.' 'Sunday the 3rd. R. works and I do some embroidery. Over breakfast we discuss *Hamlet*.' As one might guess, one of Wahnfried's favourite Shakespearean plays was *The Merchant of Venice*. As was quite frequently the case, Wagner read out the play to his family circle – 'and R. put into words the amazement which we all felt at the fact that it was three hundred years ago that the poet had described precisely the same type as that with which we ourselves are still being so unpleasantly confronted today.' It is not surprising that Wagner should have felt such a close affinity towards Shakespeare. It was not just that his literary taste was basically sound, but that he recognized in the English dramatist a kindred spirit, a titan who had attempted to shake the world out of its slumbers, a gigantomane who saw nothing amiss in writing a work of art which lasted several evenings (*Henry VI*, Parts I to III), a mysterious artist whose works, like Wagner's own, could be interpreted in a thousand different ways.

Wagner's *Parsifal* has even been cited by animal protection societies–'Du konntest morden? Hier im heil'gen Walde?' ('How could you murder? Here in the sacred forest?'). 'Levi quotes us a passage from *Cymbeline*, which could serve as a motto against vivisection. "Shakespeare contains literally everything!" R. calls out, delightedly.' Once the book had been closed, whether it be by Homer, Goethe, Calderón or Shakespeare, conversation soon turned once again to the Jews; it always went back to the Jews. 'Personally, I include Jews among my closest friends,' Wagner used to say. 'But it was wrong of us to give them the chance to become emancipated and grant them the same rights before we Germans ourselves were properly emancipated. The Germans are being exploited and ridiculed by the Jews, something which has turned them into lazy drunkards who want only one thing: to be just like the Jews. It has undermined their trust and faith. And who's to blame for all this? The government!'

He was so obsessed with his hatred of the Jews that he even called the North German Protestant composer, Johannes Brahms, 'a Jewish czardas-player'. Brahms, it may be added, could scarcely be seen as a rival. He had no ambitions in the field of music drama, but wrote mostly lieder, chamber music and symphonic works, areas in which Wagner was a dilettante. In spite of that–or rather precisely because of it–Brahms was viewed in Wahnfried with total abhorrence. On 19 June 1875 Cosima noted in her Diary, 'R. sent me one of the strangest letters from Herr Brahms, just as artificial and as unedifying as his compositions'. Somewhat later, on 18 November 1875, she was introduced for the first time to her husband's colleague–it is not clear from the Diaries whether Wagner himself accompanied her. It was on the occasion of a concert in which Brahms himself appeared as soloist in one of his piano quartets. 'He is a red, crude-looking man, his work is very dry and stilted.'

Fortunately, Cosima not only recorded the goings-on of the cultural giants of her own day and of the past, she also found room for her everyday cares, ranging from Fidi's nose-bleeds to Richard's constipation. 'Sunday the 26th [August 1877]. To church. R. works. First attempt to find a friend for Siegried.' 'Sunday the 2nd [December 1877]. Worried about Fidi. We've been trying to find some other boys for him to play with but he has treated them all with rudeness, vulgarity and spiteful indifference; it's terrible!'

For those of us who think of Wagner as a little man with a disproportionately large ego, it is surprising to see how depressive and insecure he could be at times. 'R. says it is sad that things have reached the point with him where he wants to hear no more of the *Nibelungenring* and that, as far as the theatre is concerned, it might just as well go up in flames.' 'If only I could write arias and duets.' 'A curse on this note-spinning ... You all imagine that it's meat and drink for me, but you're wrong.' 'What a dunce I am, I can't transpose.' 'No one will believe how bunglingly incompetent I am; I'm totally incapable of transposing. Mendelssohn would cover his eyes if he could see me composing.'

His dreams were troubled and megalomaniac by turns, although, at least while he was asleep, he had remarkably good dealings with his colleagues, especially after they were dead. In Stuttgart he once bumped into the late Carl Maria von Weber, who asked Wagner if he really felt that Weber had any musical talent. Ludwig van Beethoven came in person to invite him to attend a performance of one of his symphonies. He wandered arm in arm through the streets of Paris with no less a person than Giacomo Meyerbeer. But not even at night would he have anything to do with his severest critic, Eduard Hanslick. Wagner dreamt that the latter made an attempt at some conciliatory gesture on the occasion of a reception which they both attended. In vain. 'I'll have nothing to do with a miserable fellow like you,' he cried out.

What things must have gone on in this man's subconscious. On one occasion he dreamt he was being molested by 'two importunate Jewesses'. On another, he attended a meeting at a synagogue and on his arrival was ceremoniously greeted by two powerfully built Jews. He dreamt that, like King Lear, he wandered over the heath in rain and tempest, accompanied by the mocking sounds of his fool's singing. His sister tried to drown him and Mathilde Wesendonck tried to poison him. King Ludwig II was shot dead, while Wagner, who was of course a committed animal-lover, was bitten by a mad dog. One has the impression that Cosima's sleep was generally less troubled. In a somewhat incidental nightmare, she dreamt that Wagner was being murdered. 'By a Jew', it goes without saying.

Wagner also had his 'vain dreams' in which the King of Bavaria paid homage to him and in which the King of Prussia showered on him his professions of love. Princess Metternich set up an entire court for him. Overnight he became minister at the English court. The Queen of Prussia turned out to be his very own mother. He walked beside Goethe and conversed with Schopenhauer. He was visited by the pope (who bore a striking likeness to Anton Bruckner). 'And when R. tried to kiss his hand, His Holiness kissed his and then carried off a bottle of cognac.'

17

4

The world première of the *Ring*

One of Wagner's vain dreams came to be realized in 1876 in the shape of the world première of Wagner's tetralogy *Der Ring des Nibelungen* in his own, brand-new Festspielhaus. The event must be seen–so the poet-composer himself let it be known–as the most important event in the history of human civilization. The reaction of the public and press, however, was somewhat more muted. Eduard Hanslick, the music editor of the Vienna *Neue Freie Presse*, heard little more than 'lethal monotony', 'shrieking', 'hashish dreams' and 'rutting noises' during the whole of the sixteen hours which the music drama lasted. 'I have never before had to sit through such excruciating torment. My head threatened to burst into a thousand pieces.' In Hanslick's eyes and ears, the lowest point of all was the endless conversation between Wotan and his wife Fricka, followed by 'an autobiographical lecture covering eight full pages of text' and delivered by the supreme god himself. 'One can be certain that with the appearance of so much as the point of Wotan's spear, a half hour of emphatic boredom is in store', Hanslick wrote. But for the opera-house, which Wagner himself had designed, he had nothing but praise. A particularly good idea, in his opinion, was the darkening of the auditorium, which at that time was something of a novelty. 'For many of our fashionable Wagner-lovers, an opportunity to have forty winks without being observed was a boon whose value cannot be overestimated.'

The report of the Russian composer Peter Ilych Tchaikovsky, who had been sent to Bayreuth by the editors of the *Russky Viedomosty*, was similarly written for he most part in a minor key:

> I made a little excursion through the streets of the town. They swarmed with people of all nationalities, who looked very much preoccupied, and as if in search of something. The reason for this anxious search I discovered only too soon, as I myself had to share it. All these restless people, wandering through the town, were seeking to satisfy the pangs of hunger, which even the fullness of artistic enjoyment could not entirely assuage. The little town offers, it is true, sufficient shelter to the strangers, but it is not able to feed all its guests . . .; one can only obtain a piece of bread, or a glass of beer, with immense difficulty, by dire struggle, or cunning stratagem, or iron endurance. Even a modest place at a table, when it has been obtained, is not the end—it is then necessary to wait an eternity before the long-desired meal is served. Anarchy reigns at these meals . . .; throughout the whole duration of the festival, food forms the chief interest of the public; the artistic representations take secondary place. Cutlets, baked potatoes, omelettes—all are discussed much more eagerly than Wagner's music.

The Dutch writer Marcellus Emants represented *Het Vaderland*, the daily newspaper of The Hague. He devoted as much space to the Rheingold champagne, Wagner cigars, Fricka salmon and Tannhäuser bitters as he did to the philosophical background of the *Ring*. Here he drew attention to the study *Die Geburt der Tragödie aus dem Geiste der Musik* ('The Birth of Tragedy from the Spirit of Music'), in which the young Professor Friedrich Nietzsche had made

19

an attempt to link together the tragedies of the Greeks and the music dramas of Wagner. Emants was sceptical of this philosophical construct: 'Neither Professor Nietzsche nor Wagner himself can reconcile us to the idea of a revival of Greek tragedy. We have no more intention of enduring a return to Greek forms of art than we have of tearing down our telegraph wires and of pulling up our railway tracks.' Nietzsche himself, who at that time was still the undisputed favourite of the Holy Family, missed most of the first Festival by default. Having attended a rehearsal of *Die Walküre*, the over-sensitive philosopher took refuge in a village in the Bavarian woods, disillusioned, shocked and, above all, tormented by excruciating headaches.

The intention was that the pilgrims who came to Wagner's musico-dramatic shrine should comprise the flower of German youth and bear witness to the triumph of German art – and all, of course, free of charge. Bayreuth should not be overshadowed by 'the demonic concept of money'. The singers were graciously allowed to appear without a fee, but the audiences, in the event, were asked to pay an entrance price of 25 thalers, which automatically led to an overrepresentation of counts and earls, princes and princesses, barons and baronesses, all dressed up in furs and dripping with diamonds. They were received at a mass audience on the lawn in front of the Villa Wahnfried by a host who appeared in the guise of the antipope of music. Wagner's benefactor, King Ludwig II, was of course among the guests of honour. He had no desire to meet the other guest of honour, Emperor Wilhelm I. Also included among the high-born assembly was Dom Pedro II of Brazil who, on his arrival in Bayreuth, had been asked to complete the register in the hotel where he was staying. In the space marked 'Profession' he noted down, quite accurately, the single word 'Emperor'.

If things went somewhat awry, it was because the singers

of the time were not yet ready for the extreme demands which Wagner made on their vocal cords. At the dress rehearsal, Wagner sat groaning and moaning to such an extent that King Ludwig, who was sitting in front of him, turned round and asked anxiously whether the Master was not feeling well. Furthermore, the complexity of Wagner's stage directions wrought irrevocable havoc. And so it happened more than once that one of the 'magic stage effects' failed to work. The show-piece was to have been the complete dragon, which Wagner had had sent over from London. When it arrived, it turned out that the whole of the neck of the monster had gone astray. Musicologists suppose that the part in question was sent not to Bayreuth but to Beirut.

Nevertheless, the ageing sorcerer had brought it off, in spite of all the ridicule, scepticism and opposition which he had suffered. He addressed his guests in his own, unique way: 'You have seen what we can do; now it is up to you to further our work. And if you are prepared to do so, we shall have art.' Even by Wagner's standards, this was somewhat audaciously expressed. Had it not been art, then, that had previously been thought of as such by Bach and Mozart, Euripedes and Michelangelo? The writer Paul Lindau anticipated the sense of general disquiet: 'And so two nights ago, between 10 and 11 o'clock, the German nation gave birth to art. The mother is doing well and the father even better. Did any of those who attended the Festival dream that they were also coming to Bayreuth in order to share in the joys of childbirth?'

Thus the first Bayreuth Festival came and went. The last bar of *Götterdämmerung* died away, the last frankfurter was sold and the general public returned home by coach and rail. Eduard Hanslick met two friends of his at the entrance to the station. They all got into the same compartment and began licking their wounds. Then, as soon as the train started to move off, they fell about each other's necks with the words, 'God be praised! We've survived! It's all behind us now! The gods have faded away!'

5

Giant and gigantomane

Apart from being a giant, Wagner was also a gigantomane, whose life and works moved between grandiose gestures and major thirds. The number of characters killed in the verse drama *Leubald und Adelaïde*, which he wrote as a boy, was twenty-four, while the word 'villain' was hurled as a curse on no fewer than 104 separate occasions. Even *Rienzi*, the first of Wagner's operas which is worth taking seriously, was of such proportions that he toyed with the idea of spreading the work over two evenings, the first two acts to be given under the title *Rienzi's Grösse* ('Rienzi's Greatness') and the last three acts under the title *Rienzi's Fall* ('Rienzi's Downfall'). The plan was frustrated by audiences who refused to pay twice to see the same opera.

For Wagner, the word 'conversation' meant a monologue on his part, which sometimes lasted from six to eight hours. If ever he caught his guests engaged in a normal, friendly and open conversation and he himself, as their host, happened not to be the cynosure of all eyes, he would open his mouth and let out an inarticulate scream, and in that way ensure himself of everybody's undivided attention.

The poet and composer Peter Cornelius portrayed Wagner on stage in his opera *Der Barbier von Bagdad*, in the transparent guise of the versatile Abul Hassan Ali Ebn Becar:

> I'm an academician,
> Doctor and chemist,
> A mathematician,

Arithmetician,
As well as grammarian
And aesthetician;
Fine rhetorician,
A great historician,
An astrologer, philologist,
Physicist, geologist,
Geographer, choreographer,
Topographer, cosmographer,.
Linguist and jurist
And tourist and purist,
Painter and sculptor,
Fencer and gymnast,
Dancer and actor,
Musician and poet,
Great dramatist and epigrammatist,
Writers of satires, epics and lyrics,
As well as a latter-day Socrates
And Aristotle.
I'm a dialectician,
Sophist and eclectic,
Cynic and moral philosopher,
And Peripatetic.
I'm an athletic,
Deeply theoretic,
Thoroughly practical
Autodidactical
Universal genius:
Yes: a universal genius!

On one occasion, Peps, one of the dogs which Wagner owned during his early years in Saxony, dared to raise its voice against its master. The composer reprimanded the animal: 'What's all this then? Barking at the great Wagner?'

He produced volume upon volume of cultural theorizing, which provided an answer to *all* the questions which tormented long-suffering mankind. In his guise as philosopher, he was a typical exponent of the nineteenth-century desire for a complete, self-contained view of the world, in which everything had its proper place and function. His writings form a half-baked mishmash of one particular brand of socialism and conservatism, Hellenism and Teutonism, anti-Semitism and vegetarianism, Proudhon, Hegel, Feuerbach, Gobineau and Schopenhauer. Above all, Schopenhauer, the professional pessimist who, in the second half of the nineteenth century, provided comfort for so many of those who, in the first half of the century, had shouted out revolutionary slogans, only subsequently to see the error of their ways and to recant.

As we have since discovered, Wagner himself was not the writer and thinker for whom the world sat waiting. But it is not *all* rubbish that he committed to paper in the course of his life. His early short stories such as *Ein Ende in Paris* ('An End in Paris') and *Eine Pilgerfahrt zu Beethoven* ('A Pilgrimage to Beethoven') have an unmistakably literary quality about them. A work such as *Über das Dirigiren* ('On Conducting') still contains a good deal of sound advice about the most vain of all professions. That a book such as *Oper und Drama* ('Opera and Drama') was disfigured by his customary whining about the Jews is much to be regretted since here, too, the writer has many a true word to say about the musico-dramatic art-form which, to Wagner's dissatisfaction, had become the favourite pastime of the happy few who made only a single demand of what was being offered them: 'Tunes which fall pleasingly on the ear, nothing more'.

His later theoretical writings, on the other hand, *Die Religion und die Kunst* ('Religion and Art'), *Erkenne dich selbst* ('Know Yourself') and *Heldenthum und Christenthum* ('Heroism and Christianity'), cannot be taken seriously, even with the best will in the world. Friedrich Nietzsche was considerate enough to lay aside his pen when madness overtook him, whereas the ageing Wagner poured out his spleen more uncontrollably than ever against cock-fighting and 'American imperialism', against the blacks who were descended from apes and against meat-eating which poisoned the blood. He knew for certain that the Aryan alone was in a position to subdue the will in the spirit of Schopenhauer. And the very suggestion that Christ was a Jew was 'one of the most terrible mistakes in the whole history of the world'.

The libretti of his operas (all of which he wrote himself) are not *bad*, if set beside such musico-dramatic rattletraps as *Die Zauberflöte*, *Norma* and *La muette de Portici*. Measured against his own inordinate claims – Wagner knew for certain that he was just as great a poet as he was a composer – they are a botched job in terms of both poetic substance and dramatic eloquence.

Since the German of Goethe, Heine and Schiller was not good enough for him, he used a language of his own invention, full of words which you will not find in any dictionary. His grandson Wieland Wagner attempted, at one of his rehearsals, to translate this remarkable language into a German which would be more or less comprehensible not only to the non-German singers but to the native German-speakers as well. For some time now the bookshops in Bayreuth have had on their shelves a small dictionary intended to offer some help in decoding Wagner's texts. It is an absolutely indispensable volume, even for the advanced student. An *Allrauner*, it appears, is an all-knowing person – see Wotan. *Frieslich* = forbidding, gigantic, fearsome, frightening, baneful. A *Gauch* = a fop, fool, rogue, simpleton. A *Loskieserin* = a Valkyrie, q.v. A *Schildmaid* = a Valkyrie, as well. A *Walküre* = a warrior maid who leads to Valhalla heroes who have fallen in battle. The *Wilder Jäger* = Wotan, q.v. The *Wonnemond* = the month of May. A *Wünschmaid* is yet another word for a Valkyrie, in this particular case Wotan's dissident daughter

26

Brünnhilde. *Zergreifen, zullen, zuschmecken* and *zwicken* mean, respectively, to destroy, to suck, to taste first and to blink.

The most important feature of Wagner's texts (and after at least a century of endlessly repeated arguments, there is unfortunately no way in which I can avoid mentioning it) is the accursed *Stabreim*, or alliterative verse, which lies like mould over the surface of the libretti. Entire generations of parodists have sharpened their claws on it:

> FIRST WAGNERIAN: What a wondrous work! What weal and woe when one witnesses what welfare was in the world when Wotan wiped out all those whose witty words have called into question the worth and workings of our worshipful wishes.
> SECOND WAGNERIAN: Good God! Gladly grant I all grim-faced gall-spitters, glib-tongued gawkers and grey-haired gaffers their graceless grumbling and glossless gospel.
> THIRD WAGNERIAN: Just let them lampoon him, the loathsome liars!
> FOURTH WAGNERIAN: May the mouth of the mighty Master, manful and mild, muzzle these mumbling misanthropes.
> FIFTH WAGNERIAN: But above all else the broad belly bulging with bread and brimful of bratwurst.

Admittedly, the modest use of stylistic elements such as alliteration and internal rhyme can in principal enhance the tonal beauty of poetry and prose. But not even here can Wagner resist the temptation to exaggerate: 'Hehe! Ihr Nicker! Wie seid ihr niedlich, neidliches Volk! Aus Nibelheims Nacht naht' ich mich gern, neigtet ihr euch zu mir' ('He he! ye nixies! how ye delight me, daintiest folk! from Nibelheim's night fain would I come, would ye turn but to me!' [Frederick Jameson's translation]). Hans Mayer's unabashed and loyal defence of Wagner has my sympathy, but he is really being far too charitable when he defends Wagner's use of *Stabreim* as an attempt at some kind of 'alienation effect' avant la lettre. If Wagner's *Stabreim* alienates us from anything, it is from the music drama to which it seeks to give poetical support. It is an aesthetic *evil* and one of the reasons why many opera-goers breathe a sigh of relief when everything finally goes quiet on stage and the orchestra can get on with depicting the Entry of the Gods into Valhalla.

Wagner said, 'May the highest truth be our dogma'. This was a rule of conduct which he daily contravened. Except where artistic matters were concerned. As an *artist*, Wagner was forward-looking and incorruptible. We do well to remember just how conservative the musical life of his own time was: women sat in the stalls eating their sandwiches, while the men generally stumbled into their seats after the second act had already started; the boxes had curtains across them which were drawn when their occupants wished to amuse themselves in some other way; the music on stage was insubstantial, cobbled together by composers such as Auber, Adam and Halévy; orchestras could play only *mezzoforte*, not having heard anything that was *piano* or *fortissimo*.

Wagner's stage-works are a long declaration of war addressed to the traditional world of opera and there was no one who could force him into making an artistic compromise. In Munich he arranged a 'model performance' of *Lohengrin*, casting his old friend Joseph Tichatschek in the title-role. Vocally, this artist was a swan-knight who left nothing to be desired, but outwardly he dragged around the stage an enormous beer-belly on the grand scale. For King Ludwig II who, in his naive way, tended to identify with the figure of Lohengrin, there was no question about it: this 'knight of the doleful countenance' would have to be replaced by another singer. Wagner refused, in spite of the fact that it was in his interest not to anger the king; instead of which, he threw his beret into the ring.

It was at a private concert for this same King Ludwig that the Munich Court Orchestra performed the Prelude to *Parsifal* under the composer's direction. At the end, the king let it be known that he desired to hear the work a second time. The piece was duly repeated, though with little enthusiasm, since Wagner thought his music too good for a programme of Family Favourites. Ludwig then demanded to hear the Prelude to *Lohengrin*, whereupon Wagner, pale with anger, threw down his baton and stormed out of the theatre. Even during the preceding period, before Wagner became Europe's most famous composer, his behaviour had been just the same. The French première of *Tannhäuser* in 1861 brought him into conflict with the directors of the Paris Opéra. In keeping with local operatic tradition, they demanded that Wagner should compose a special ballet for the second act. This was the moment when the gentlemen of the so-called Jockey Club, who were in the habit of dining quite late, would enter their boxes and from there, feeling agreeably full and flushed with the wine which they had drunk with their meal and the cognac which had followed, they would delight in the swaying bosoms and corybantic limbs of the corps de ballet. Wagner condemned the idea: there was no room for a ballet in his conception of the second act. This led to what Robert Gutman called one of 'the most shameful events in France's musical history'. The Jockey Club had had dog-whistles specially made with the inscription 'Pour Tannhäuser' engraved on them and with these they ruined the first series of performances with the noise of their cat-calls, laughter and hissing. A second series was prevented from taking place. Wagner withdrew his score and demanded that no further performances of the work should be given. Three weeks later there appeared Charles Baudelaire's famous pamphlet, *Richard Wagner et le*

'Tannhäuser' à Paris, in which the poet predicted, 'Those people who think they have destroyed Wagner are premature in their expressions of delight'.

It is true that even the libretto of such a work as *Tannhäuser* ('Hoch über aller Welt ist Gott, und sein Erbarmen ist kein Spott' ['High over all the world is God, and His great mercy is not mockery']) cannot be read without raised eyebrows. But his libretti remain interesting for their pre-Freudian insights into the meaning of dreams, symbols and unspoken feelings of a mostly sexual nature. Here, too, Wagner reveals himself as an artist who pushed back the frontiers of art. What taboos, for example, did he break down when, at the end of Act I of *Die Walküre*, he had the twins Siegmund and Sieglinde incestuously sleeping together, the whole action accompanied by a text which left nothing to the imagination: 'Braut und Schwester bist du dem Bruder–so blühe denn Wälsungenblut!' ('Bride and sister are you to your brother–so let the blood of the Volsungs flourish!')?

Murder and violent death were familiar ingredients in the operas of the time. But to put adultery and incest upon the stage, as Wagner did, on a grand scale, was bound to be seen as an outright provocation. Fortunately, Wagner was generally inclined to express himself somewhat unclearly, so that even today most members of the audience are unaware of the fact, for example, that (according to Robert Gutman) *Tristan und Isolde* is really a homosexual *roman à clef* centred around the triangular relationship of Tristan, Marke and Melot. It is not for nothing that a *deus ex machina* is necessary in the form of a love-potion before Tristan and Isolde finally fall into each other's arms after a prelude of some three-quarters of an hour, 'ungetrennt, ewig einig, ohne End, ohn Erwachen, ohn Erbarmen, namenlos, in Lieb' umfangen' ('undivided, eternally united, without end, without waking, without mercy, nameless, embraced by love').

I have the very definite impression that, if they really knew what they were watching so demurely, many Wagnerians would get up and leave the Festspielhaus in high dudgeon, holding their fingers to their noses.

Who am I to condemn the sensuous figure of Kundry? But it remains a fact that she attempts to get Parsifal into bed with her, luring the pure fool on by appealing to the name of his *mother*. Or take the third act of *Siegfried*. Scarcely has the hero made the acquaintance of his aunt Brünnhilde when he confesses to her (again appealing to his mother) that his blood seethes with growing desire. Even such a refreshingly youthful work as *Der fliegende Holländer*, we learn from a recent publication (Isolde Vetter, *Senta und der Holländer : eine narzisstische Kollusion mit tödlichem Ausgang* ['Senta and the Dutchman : a narcissistic collusion with fatal outcome']), is really a psycho-analytical piece of high-class pornography. The so-called 'homeland', for which the Dutchman longs, symbolizes none other than his desire to return to a lost state of archetypal harmony, the early, pre-natal union with the mother. His prayer to perish beneath the waves similarly points in the direction of a fixation with the mother's womb, whereby attention may be drawn to the common Indo-European root of the words *wave* in English, *Welle* in German and *vulva* in Latin. In other words, the Festspielhaus at Bayreuth ought to be under the surveillance not only of the local fire brigade but under that of the vice squad as well.

As should be obvious, this sort of interpretation deserves to be regarded with a certain sense of irony. If you look hard enough and juggle with the right psycho-analytical concepts, even Bach's *Saint Matthew Passion* appears to teem with sexual innuendo. Yet it cannot be denied that there runs through Wagner's works just as clear an undercurrent of eroticism as there does through his private life. I have certainly no intention of going sniffing under his bed-clothes; it is enough to note the fact that he exercised a quite astounding fascination on all those around him, whether it was Cosima von Bülow or Hans von Bülow, Mathilde Wesendonck or Otto Wesendonck. Wagner was in a position to pop over into Otto Wesendonck's living room whenever he was in need of what I might call (and again I am doing my utmost to find a decent expression) an intimate *tête-à-tête* with the latter's wife. More than that, Wesendonck was ready at any given moment voluntarily to relinquish his rights as a man and as a husband, so that his over-sensitive visitor should not feel put out.

Wagner was an extremely philogynistic artist—and, for their part, women had a weakness for the small, fiery, talkative trouble-maker. That, Wagner said, was because women, contrary to the prevailing view, had not yet sunk so low as to shield their souls as thoroughly as was the case with men. Here, too, Wagner was correct. But the number of his affairs was actually quite small. In all, there were about six or seven which, spread out over half-a-century, cannot be called excessive. I have the impression that it was not so much his love-life which enjoyed the principal attention of the petty bourgeoisie as his unbridled passion for frills, dark green shirts, pink underwear, artificial purple roses, bright red socks, chamois shirts and lilac-coloured cloth.

'Ah God,' he wrote to a passing flame, 'how I'm looking forward to being able to rest beside you by and by (I hope the pink knickers are ready?). Yes! Just be nice and kind to me! I do deserve to be spoiled again for just a little while.' This sort of inclination on Wagner's part led his contemporaries to feel convinced that, at the very least, they were dealing with a fetishist and a homosexual transvestite with feminine leanings. My own view is that his passion for frilly things reveals a need to show off on the part of a social upstart, coloured by the bad taste of the age. And who are we to criticise Wagner's pink underwear—we who are children of a century in which erotic satisfaction is sought on a grand scale in bubble-baths with massage at the management's discretion?

In spite of this, present-day Wagnerians are still inclined to gloss over this most innocent of Wagner's pleasures. In 1967 there appeared a most remarkable book entitled *Richard Wagner and the milliner : or, The long arm of libel*, by the Wagner scholar Ludwig Kusche. It dealt with the fate of the letters which Wagner wrote over a period of years to Bertha Goldwag, a Viennese dealer in fabrics, who provided him with all his multi-coloured silks, velvet and bombazine. Even before Wagner's death, their correspondence fell into the hands of the satirist of the *Neue Freie Presse*, which promptly published the material in serialized form. A century later Kusche can still not get over his sense of outrage : 'The world is fond of sensationalism, indiscretions and gossip'. Who—he asks—could begrudge Wagner his lilac-coloured bedspreads? When has journalism or scholarship ever looked into the compromising fact that Arthur Schopenhauer gained his best insights in the smallest room of his flat in Frankfurt? After all, no one would claim that *Die Welt als Wille und Vorstellung* ('The World as Will and Imagination') stinks of human faeces. Moreover, the author goes on, we are dealing in Wagner's case with 'private letters whose contents are of no concern to Wagner's contemporaries nor to our own' (the second half of the book in question contains *all* the milliner's letters that Kusche could lay his hands on).

Apart for his passion for silks and for the wives of his benefactors, there was a third love in Wagner's life : he was a committed animal-lover. This is something that needs to be expressly stated, in a world which still speaks so ill of the composer. The Wagner expert Leo Fremgen, whom I should have brought in sooner as a witness for the defence, has drawn attention in his essay *Richard Wagner's Love of Animals : one aspect of his humanitarianism* (1977) to the central role which Fips, Peps, Robber, Pohl, Russ and their descendants Marke, Brange, Kunde, Froh, Fricka and Freia played in the Master's life. 'It would be good to linger a moment over this aspect of Wagner instead of condemning the great man for his silk pyjamas, his carpets, his perfume bottles and his love affairs.'

During the winter of 1862–1863, Wagner was bitten in the hand by a bulldog, whose name we have not been able to ascertain. As a result his master was unable to compose for some time. 'But his love of the animal in question remained undiminished.' Fremgen speaks with repugnance of 'certain scholars of extremist views' who, addressed by Wagner the anti-vivisectionist on the subject of the bad publicity which their tormenting of rabbits for experimental purposes was likely to have, had had the temerity to reply that at least there were a few things which were still sacred, compared to the drawbacks of living in the neighbourhood of a *conservatory*. Wagner's love of animals, according to the writer, finds clear expression in his dramatic works, especially in *Parsifal*, in which the leading character is bitterly reproached for his having killed a swan, but above all in the *Ring* with its floundering fish and warbling woodbirds : 'Es sangen die Vöglein, so selig im Lenz' ('The little birds sang, so blissful in spring').

As one can see, this is Wagnerian exegesis on a remarkable level. The fact that the author omits to mention the cruel butchery of Fafner the dragon, to say nothing of the manner in which Brünnhilde's stallion, Grane, is urged into the flames for no good reason, in no way detracts from Wagner's fundamental love of everything that stirs in wood and pasture.

6

A socialist who hated socialists

The fact that for decades the Green Hill was a place of pilgrimage for the blackest of reactionaries should not allow us to forget that Wagner was a progressive individual, politically as well as artistically.

His autobiography *Mein Leben* considerably trivializes his involvement in the bourgeois revolution of 1848–1849 and his later house-biographers had a similarly dismissive attitude towards his socio-critical activities. But there is no doubt that, if he had been alive today, Wagner would have been excluded from holding public office by governmental decree, on the grounds of his highly dubious loyalty to the 'basic order of free democracy'. He may reasonably be labelled a member of the politico-literary school known as 'Young Germany', a movement critical of society and led by such *Heimatlose Linken* (literally, 'Homeless Left-wingers') as Heinrich Laube, Karl Gutzkow, Heinrich Heine and Ludolf Wienbarg. The Young German movement was formally outlawed on 14 November 1835 on the grounds of 'its crude undermining of the Christian religion, its calling into question of existing social structures and its denial of discipline and morality'. The result was a long list of forbidden publications, which included even Dante's *Divine Comedy*, because, said the censor, divine matters were not suitable material for a comedy.

Wagner at this time was firmly convinced that Germany, with its many princes, was ripe for revolution. But someone was needed to put the match to the powder-barrel and blow up the old, decaying regime. On 15 June in the revolutionary year 1848 he addressed the *Vaterlandsverein* in Dresden, calling upon its members : 'Do not give alms, but acknowledge the right, the God-given human right; for, if you do not, you will live to see the day when nature, who has been so brutally despised, arms herself for a bitter conflict, whose savage cry of victory will be that of communism . . . Do you think these are idle threats? No! They are a warning to us all!'

The composer declared himself to be an advocate of the abolition of the First Chamber as well as of the aristocracy. But the king could remain, as 'the first of the republicans'. The composer was evidently a revolutionary of a somewhat remarkable kind, a revolutionary who, apart from being a monarchist, was also an imperialist; and so he demanded that Germany, too, should get hold of a few colonies to dispose of. 'We shall do it better than the Spaniards, for whom the New World became a sanctimonious slaughterhouse, and better than the English, who turned it into a grocer's shop.' The Old World noticed this when it finally reached that stage just one short century later.

Wagner was a socialist who hated socialists. He was against progress, as manifested in the industrialization of society, and he saw culture—not politics—as the moral foundation of society. Revolution, he thought, was the means which would put the common people in a position to be able to listen, free-of-charge, to lofty music dramas—*his* music dramas, which would be subsidized by the king or by the emperor in opera-houses where he, Wagner, would have complete control. 'A single sensible resolve on the part of the King of Prussia with regard to his opera-houses and everything would be set to rights again.'

There was as much missionary zeal as there was naiveté in Wagner's vision of the role which art could play in public life. 'The socialist and the federalist,' writes Martin Gregor-Dellin, 'the revolutionary and the poet of martial and patriotic verse – this man was not really a political agitator nor an opportunistic fellow traveller, but a failed redeemer : Lohengrin the Second.' Certain writers have remained suspicious and supposed that it was less Wagner the revolutionary than Wagner the debtor who wanted to change society, because he set out from the belief that, as capitalist society went up in flames, so, too, would the mountainous pile of unpaid bills.

His *Collected Works* include a fragmentary sketch which, among other things, includes the words, 'A violent movement passes through the world. It is the storm of European revolution. Every one of us is implicated in it and he who does not actively support it, stands in its way.' One does not need to be an expert in historical materialism to be able to work out the intellectual parentage of these ideas. As late as 1872, eleven years before Wagner's death, we have record of a remark in which, however grotesque it may sound, he described himself as 'a communist'. By 'communism' Wagner understood something completely different from what was intended by the 'doctors of the revolution', Marx and Engels. Wagner had no sympathy whatsoever for the liquidization of private property, still less was he an advocate of the proletarian revolution. Throughout his whole life his political philosophy could be summarized in no more than three words: 'Property is theft', a point of view borrowed from Pierre-Joseph Proudhon's *De la propriété*. He remained loyal to this view throughout his entire life. Surrounded by the palazzi of Venice, where he was later to die, he cried out, 'This is property! The source of all evil!'

Even Wagner's anti-Semitism, one fears, was based in part upon sentiments which were mistakenly thought of as being revolutionary. Just like such kindred spirits and 'true socialists' as Proudhon, Fourier and Lamennais, Wagner, too, was inclined to generalize on the basis of the Rothschilds' stock-exchange dealings and hence to curse the entire capitalist system. The views of his contemporary comrade-in-arms, Heinrich Heine, who had fled to Paris following the ban on the works of the Young German writers, were noticeably less dogmatic. The fact that Heine, too, was susceptible to the lure of socialism was no reason for him not to be 'famillionair' (as he put it) with the Rothschild family.

It will come as unwelcome news to Bayreuth's regular visitors, but as a social insurrectionist Wagner really represents the ultra-left-wing, popular Marxist, anti-worker, *terrorist* tradition of European socialism, the socialism of action, beginning with Blanqui, continuing with Bakunin and Buonarotti and ending, one hopes, with the Baader-Meinhof group. One should read what he wrote to a friend on 30 December 1851:

> My entire politics consists of nothing but the bloodiest hatred for our whole civilization ... I must now atone for thinking so highly of workers as workers. With all their clamour about labour, they are the most miserable of slaves whom anybody may pocket who promises them a lot of 'work' at the moment. It all stems from our servile attitude; no one in all France knows that we are *human*, except perhaps Proudhon, and even he not clearly! But in all of Europe I prefer dogs to those doglike men. Yet I don't despair of a better future, only the most terrific and destructive Revolution could make our civilized beasts 'human' again.

It has never been possible to prove for certain that Wagner himself was responsible for the fire which destroyed the Dresden Opera. But that he was capable of doing so is clear from the poem *Die Not* ('Need'), which he wrote at the time of the revolution:

> The fire-brand, ha! Let it burn
> Brightly, broadly and widely,
> Let it reduce to ashes all those places
> Which are dedicated to the worship of Mammon!

In his autobiography Wagner describes how, while in Dresden, he fell under the dominating influence of the exiled anarchist Michael Bakunin, who explained to him that the true enemies of progress were not so much tyrants as the petty bourgeoisie. 'As a typical example of the latter he proposed the Protestant pastor who refuses to believe in himself as a human being until he himself has set fire to his vicarage, with his wife and child inside it ... He had no wish to find out more about my Nibelung studies. Inspired by my reading of the Gospels, I had at that time sketched out the scenario for a tragedy "Jesus of Nazareth", intended for the ideal stage of the future ... As for the music, Bakunin recommended that I should limit myself to setting a single text, infinitely varied: the tenor should sing, "Off with his head!", the soprano "Hang him!" and the *basso continuo* "Fire, fire!"'

This is a principle to which Wagner remained loyal even in the years when his revolutionary ardour had begun to cool. He remained an intellectual terrorist throughout his entire life. The mere mention of the name of Paris was sufficient for him to give his destructive fantasies free reign. 'With total sobriety and in all seriousness,' he wrote to Theodor Uhlig on 22 October 1850, 'I assure you that I no longer believe in any other revolution except that which begins with the burning down of Paris.' The same picture emerges from entries in Cosima's Diaries dating from the first few days of the Franco-Prussian War. 'Wednesday the

2nd [November 1870]. Paris is being bombarded. What did I tell you?–as the saying goes . . . Friday the 4th [November 1870]. Rumours of a truce; much to our annoyance. R. wants the city to be bombarded.' Wagner would never forgive the Parisians for having booed *Tannhäuser*.

The scenario of Wagner's most elaborate work, which at that time was still called 'Die Nibelungensage', was completed on 4 October 1848. The libretto of *Der Ring des Nibelungen*, based upon it, was ready by the end of 1852. Wagner's tetralogy is thus undeniably a poetical by-product of his years as a revolutionary and must therefore be interpreted as a *socialist* work of art–yet another idea which is not likely to go down well on the Green Hill.

This interpretation was put forward as early as 1898 by Bernard Shaw in his thought-provoking essay, *The Perfect Wagnerite*. It is a tragedy, says the music critic Joachim Kaiser, that this piece has never been taken seriously, either by Wagnerians or by anti-Wagnerians. For, if it had been, Wagner would never have been annexed by the Nazis, and his socio-critical detractors would not have had cause to denounce him politically. The foundations for Shaw's study were laid in the reading-room of the British Library, where a good deal else has been hatched, besides. Shaw could be found there, every day, poring over two books simultaneously, Marx's *Das Kapital* and the score of Wagner's *Tristan und Isolde*.

The *Ring*, Shaw believed, is a radical socialist parable on the curse of gold. Siegfried is Wagner's ill-considered friend, Bakunin, in disguise; the dark caves in which the Nibelungs forge their swords are the poetical reflex of the unchecked, early-capitalist, nineteenth-century establishment. Even the famous *Tarnhelm*, by means of which the dwarf Alberich performs his conjuring tricks, is subjected by Shaw to a materialistic interpretation: 'This helmet is a very common article in our streets, where it generally takes the form of a tall hat. It makes a man invisible as a shareholder, and changes him into various shapes, such as a pious Christian, a subscriber to hospitals, a benefactor of the poor, a model husband and father, a shrewd, practical, independent Englishman, and what not, when he is really a pitiful parasite on the commonwealth, consuming a great deal, and producing nothing, feeling nothing, knowing nothing, believing nothing and doing nothing.'

After having been ignored for almost three-quarters of a century, the justness of Shaw's interpretation has finally been confirmed by the publication of Cosima's Diaries: 'The other day R. said that it gave him pleasure to have offered in the *Ring* a complete picture of the curse of greed, together with the ruin which it entails.'

In the meantime, Wagnerians had subjected the *Ring* to theosophical, cosmological, metaphysical, Old Germanic and psycho-analytical interpretations. There is even a juridical interpretation, published in 1968 by an author described as a lawyer under the title *Richard Wagner's Ring des Nibelungen in the light of German Civil Law*. Wagner's alleged masterpiece, the author convincingly demonstrates, is really a Wanted List set to music. Alberich deserves life imprisonment for theft and incitement to murder. Fafner deserves the same for abduction and murder. Siegfried deserves fifteen years' imprisonment for manslaughter, abduction and cruelty to animals. Brünnhilde deserves life imprisonment for incitement to murder, as well as for arson; and Wotan, the chief god, deserves fifteen years for murder, manslaughter, arson and unlawfully administering anaesthetizing drugs.

How is it then that, in spite of all this, the *Ring* is never really exciting? I believe the reason lies in the fact that the poet-composer has arrogantly ignored the most basic rules

41

of music drama. Once again he has sworn by monologues which last at least half-an-hour and dialogues of at least three-quarters of an hour's duration, and throughout all this not a leaf stirs on stage. The popularity of the *Ring*, one fears, is less a question of artistic merit than of propaganda. If you compose an opera which, in length, comes close to rivalling Mozart's complete dramatic output, and if you then draw this opera out over four whole evenings, people it with giants, dwarfs, gods and a roaring dragon, underpin it all with a sort of private - philosophy, build a theatre especially for it, ensure yourself of royal patronage and demand inflated entrance prices – then the audience should be convinced that they are participating in a cultural event of unique importance.

This has remained the case right up until today. Who dares to assert that the famous *Ring* comes to life only intermittently, as in the first act of *Die Walküre* and the third act of *Siegfried*, but that the work as a whole includes insufficient musical and dramatic material to be able to hold the audience's attention over a period of sixteen hours?

Nor is it Wagner's most *sympathetic* work. Once again, the composer's anti-intellectualism is quite striking. The gods have blessed Siegfried with every quality apart from intellect. The dwarfs Mime and Alberich, on the other hand, are disposed to make good use of their grey matter, which is something for which they finally have to pay. In his essay *Versuch über Wagner*, Theodor W. Adorno put forward the thesis that Alberich and Mime, at the deepest level, are Jewish caricatures. The former Adorno describes as 'obsessed with gold, invisibly anonymous and quick to exploit others', while Mime is described as 'shoulder-shrugging, garrulous and bubbling over with self-praise and cunning deceit'. I had long regarded this as a somewhat speculative claim, but closer examination of the text makes me think that after all Adorno was not so very wide of the mark. In the first draft of the *Ring* scenario in 1848, Wagner described the Nibelungs as beings who moved through the bowels of the earth like 'vermin' in a dead body. It is an image which returns in Wagner's essay on *Das Judenthum in der Musik* ('Judaism in Music') of 1850. There it is the Jews who, for their part, are likened to vermin: 'only in real life can we, too, rediscover the spirit of art, not in its vermin-infested corpse'.

Fortunately Wagner is not at his best as a satirist, so that not even the Nazis appreciated this deeper layer of meaning. Mime and Alberich, in any case, are simply failures as caricatures. In spite of all that the text suggests to the contrary, the audience ultimately feels sorry for the pitiful Alberich, who pays for the rape of the Rhinegold with his inability ever again to enjoy love. This is even truer of Mime: he is treated so insensitively by Wagner that by the end of the opera he is assured of all our sympathies. Admittedly, he won't stop talking and he is a rather unpleasant character. But is that any reason to put him in fear of his life by setting a savage bear on him ('Friss ihn! Friss ihn, den Fratzenschmied! Hahahahahahahahahaha!' ['Eat him! Eat him, the grimacing smith! Hahahahaha-hahahaha!']), to insult him ('Garstiger Gauch! Schänd-licher Stümper! Ekliger Schwätzer!' ['Loathsome fool! Shameful bungler! Disgusting babbler!']) and finally to stab him mercilessly?

Something which is emphatically not true of such operas as *Parsifal* and *Tristan und Isolde* is, in my own opinion, true of the *Ring*. The latter work is most successful when the singers are silent. The Prelude to *Die Walküre*, Siegfried's Rhine Journey, the Ride of the Valkyries and Siegfried's Funeral March, all show Wagner at his unparalleled best. The duet between Brünnhilde and Waltraute, on the other hand, is infinitely protracted and over-blown. And yet it

must be admitted that no one was better able than Wagner
to set to music the end of the world, which is what happens
in the final pages of *Götterdämmerung*:

> She has leapt impetuously on to her horse and
> spurs it on with a single leap into the burning pile
> of logs . . .; the waters of the Rhine have swollen
> and burst their banks, so that its flood-waters
> pour over the scene of the fire . . . Hagen is seized
> with utter panic at the sight of the Rhinemaidens;
> he hurriedly throws down his spear, shield and
> helmet and plunges like a madman into the flood
> . . . Woglinde and Wellgunde place their arms
> around his neck and swim backwards, dragging
> him down with them into the depths: Flosshilde,
> at their head, exultantly holds aloft the recap-
> tured ring . . . From the ruins of the fallen hall the
> men and women watch with profound emotion as
> the flames leap up high into the sky. When the
> glow reaches its brightest intensity, the hall of
> Valhalla suddenly becomes visible, with the gods
> and heroes all assembled there. Bright flames
> seem to seize upon the hall of the gods. As the
> gods become entirely hidden by the flames, the
> curtain falls.

If Wagner had lived a century later, his home would not
have been Bayreuth but Beverly Hills, and he would not
have written music dramas, let alone a *Bühnenweihfestspiel*,
but the sound-tracks for disaster movies such as *Earthquake*
and *The Towering Inferno*.

7

Friedrich Nietzsche
and the fascination of *Tristan*

Practising Wagnerians, according to Herbert Rosendorfer, swear by the *Ring*. Those whose speciality is *Parsifal* are for the most part zealots of the strictest orthodoxy. *Die Meistersinger von Nürnberg* is the favourite opera of the German National infantry. 'But if anyone claims *Tristan und Isolde* as Wagner's most important work, caution is advisable, because one is dealing either with a woman who is seeking a cultural substitute for eroticism or religion, or else with a connoisseur who is alive to the historically epochmaking character of the work.'

The excitable pianola-player Edmund Pfühl in Thomas Mann's *Buddenbrooks* symbolizes the complete sense of disorientation which this opera can have on an oversensitive nature:

> I cannot play it, Frau Buddenbrooks; I am your obedient servant, but I cannot play it. It is not music–believe me ... I have always imagined that I knew something about music! This is chaos! It is demagogy, blasphemy and sheer madness! It is a perfume-scented haze shot through with flashes of lightning. It is the end of all morality in art! I won't play it! ... Forgive me, Frau Buddenbrooks, if I speak so candidly ... You pay my fees, you have been paying for my services for a long time now ... and I am a man of modest means. But I shall resign, I shall throw up everything if you force me to commit

such a godless act ... And the child sitting there
on his chair! He has slipped in to listen to some
music! Do you want to poison his mind utterly?

For all this, *Tristan und Isolde* is Wagner's most modest as
well as his least pretentious musico-dramatic work. In its
conception and casting, the opera was intended as a mere
trifle, written as a short-term attempt to defer his most
pressing financial obligations. Decor and costumes are
simple. The number of main characters is manageable. For
the same reason – and unlike the cost-intensive *Tannhäuser* –
it has remained the favourite opera of Bayreuth's ac-
countants for just on a century. As far as the plot is
concerned, the work is untypical of Wagner in that it is not
wholly devoid of logic. Authentic emotions are expressed by
real people who bear no resemblance to the shaggy-haired,
Germanic types with whom Wagner is normally indentified.
Not a single German appears on stage throughout the entire
work, since the legend on which the libretto is based is
Celto-Romance in origin.

From the point of view of its harmony, the Prelude to Act
I is one of the most daring compositions of the nineteenth
century. The duet in Act II (something which Wagner
rarely ventured to write) is pure passion turned into music.
Isolde's Transfiguration with which the opera ends belongs
to some of the most moving pages in the whole of operatic
literature.

Yes, indeed – *operatic* literature. *Tristan und Isolde* is not a
music drama, nor a *Bühnenweihfestspiel* and certainly not a
Gesamtkunstwerk. It is an *opera* and one which, moreover,
turned out so successful that it simultaneously spelt the
bankruptcy of many of Wagner's over-blown theories.

I shall withdraw into the background for a moment in
order to make room for expert witnesses. Giacomo Puccini
once played fragments of *Tristan* to a friend of his for hours

on end; finally he slammed the score shut with a gesture of annoyance and said, 'Compared to this, we're a wretched band of dilettantes and mandoline-strummers'. The young Arturo Toscanini was himself busy writing an opera when a copy of the score of *Tristan* fell into his hands. As a result he destroyed everything which he had already committed to paper. 'This is the opera of all operas. I shall have achieved nothing until I have breathed new life into this work.' The young Bruno Walter scraped together enough money from his limited means in order to buy a ticket for *Tristan*: 'And so there I sat in the topmost gallery of the Berlin Opera and from the very first entry of the 'cellos I felt my heart contract ... I was no longer of this world. At the end I wandered aimlessly through the streets and when I got home I said nothing and asked to be left alone. The song of ecstasy continued to vibrate within me the whole night long, and when I woke up the next morning, I knew that the world was a changed place.'

Wagner, too, was aware that he was producing an exceptional work of art, even while he was still composing it: 'Child!' he wrote to Mathilde Wesendonck on 10 April 1859. 'This Tristan is turning into something *terrible*! This final act!!! I'm afraid the opera will be banned—unless the whole thing be parodied by a bad performance—: only mediocre performances can save me! Perfectly *good* ones are bound to drive people insane—I can't imagine it otherwise.'

The sixteen-year-old Friedrich Nietzsche and the other members of the Germania Debating Society had clubbed together in order to be able to buy a copy of the piano score of *Tristan und Isolde*. Many years later he called down curses on all of Wagner's works, with the single exception of this opera which had been his boyhood passion. 'Even now I am still in search of a work which exercises such a dangerous fascination, such a spine-tingling and blissful infinity as *Tristan*—I have sought in vain, in every art.'

47

Cosima referred to Nietzsche by name for the first time on 17 May 1869. She reports that the family had enjoyed a 'peaceful and agreeable' visit from the philologist, Professor Nietzsche, 'who has a profound knowledge of R.'s works'. Wagner, who was thirty-one years older and two heads shorter than his new friend, treated the young professor with the greatest cordiality. There was a never-ending stream of idol-worshippers, *décadents*, anti-Semites and over-excitable marchionesses, virtually trampling down the Wagners' front door; but until now a real, live *scholar* had not been part of the court.

Nietzsche fell deeply under the influence of Wagner's charm, vitality, eloquence and breadth of reading. 'What I learn and see, hear and understand here is indescribable: Schopenhauer and Goethe, Aeschylus and Pindar are still alive, believe me.' For his own part, Wagner was delighted with his no less brilliant admirer. 'I swear to you by God,' he told him, 'that I regard you as the only person who understands what I want.' Cosima, too, was amused by the serious young man. In fact, Nietzsche told her, he was descended from a family of Polish counts. 'What a shame,' replied his hostess, dryly. 'I'd find you much more interesting if you were the son of some unpretentious Thuringian clergyman.'

Two rooms were soon permanently set aside for Nietzsche, as were his host's evenings, which were devoted to discussions about Wagner's philosophy of music–'which makes it therefore the *only* philosophy of music', the apprentice wrote in a letter to the Master. The two men both saw music as the mother of Greek tragedy and as the opposite of the accursed 'theoretical man', embodied in Socrates, the conscious artist and enemy of instinct. Wagner had found scope in his works for the elemental forces of Dionysus, and it was thanks to this (Nietzsche suspected and Wagner knew for certain) that the composer would become the spirit of a new, anti-Socratic, anti-Christian culture. At a later date, on the eve of the première of the *Ring*, Nietzsche was to realize that Wagner's veneration of antiquity had to be taken with a decent pinch of Attic salt.

Nietzsche's name appears at regular intervals in Cosima's Diaries during the years from 1869 to 1876. 'In the afternoon, visit from Pr. Nietzsche who tells me that it is quite unbelievable what lies are being printed about R. and circulating in the world (such as, for example, the way in which he stands in front of the mirror in order to form a counterpart to Goethe and Schiller–then about his love of luxury, his harem, his intimacy with the King of Bavaria, whom he corrupts with all his perversities, etc.). We wonder what sort of a picture posterity will gain of him.' But relations were not always as harmonious as this. 'Coffee with Pr. Nietzsche: unfortunately he upsets R. very much by reason of the vow which he has made not to eat meat, but only vegetarian food. R. regards this as arrogant nonsense and when the prof. tells him that it is a matter of ethical importance as well, not to eat animals etc., R. replies that our whole existence is a compromise.'

Nietzsche of course made regular use of his hosts' piano. 'No, Nietzsche! You play much too well for a man of learning', Wagner told him.

Wagner was concerned about Nietzsche's immoderate fear of the opposite sex. 'I think', the composer said, 'that you must either get married or else write an opera. Marriage strikes me as the better alternative.' On one occasion Nietzsche was invited to accompany Professor Karl Mendelssohn-Bartholdy on a journey to Greece. He prudently informed Cosima of the fact. She replied by return of post: 'The son of Felix! It is most curious. I think I know what your decision will be.' And so Nietzsche remained at home.

The Wagners nevertheless noticed to their dismay that

their protégé had begun to show an increasing tendency towards apodictic utterances and naughty behaviour. In 1870, when Wilhelm I had been proclaimed emperor, Wagner had marked the event by writing a *Kaisermarsch*, while his rival, Johannes Brahms, had composed a *Triumphlied* for the same occasion. It was this very same *Triumphlied* which Nietzsche brought with him when he visited Wahnfried in the summer of 1874. His host felt it as a bitter insult. 'I was well aware that Nietzsche was trying to say: "Just look, here is somebody else who is also capable of writing something worthwhile!" Well, a few evenings later I exploded. And how!' Nietzsche listened to the outburst 'dumbfounded, but with a decent show of dignity'. 'No,' he used to say later, whenever the incident was referred to again, 'on that occasion Wagner was not great.'

Nietzsche's essay *Richard Wagner in Bayreuth* appeared shortly before the 1876 Bayreuth Festival. The work was openly friendly towards the composer, but the critical undertow of the prose pointed clearly to the fact that the philosopher had already left behind him his earlier stage of blind admiration. Was Wagner perhaps 'not the prophet of the future which he claimed to be, but a man who has interpreted and transfigured the past'? The friendship between the two men was only briefly to survive the première of the *Ring*. Nietzsche felt a sense of disgust at the pomp and circumstance which surrounded the Green Hill. 'It was as though I was dreaming ... But where was I? I recognized nothing, I scarcely recognized Wagner.' According to Julius Kapp (*Richard Wagner: eine Biographie*, 1910), not only was there a growing artistic and philosophical gulf between the two men, there was also a 'particular reason' for the break. This emerges, says Kapp, from a letter which Wagner sent to Nietzsche's doctor in 1877, a letter which 'it would be inappropriate to publish in view of the sensitive nature of its contents'. Modern Wagner scholarship fortunately suffers from fewer scruples than Kapp did, with the result that we now know that Wagner had let it be known that Nietzsche's alarming physical condition was attributable (in his opinion) to excessive masturbation, for which reason he recommended cold water treatment by way of a cure. Nietzsche soon learned of this attempt at diagnosis and spoke furiously of 'perfidy' and 'mortal insults'.

He is fortunate not to have lived long enough to have had to put up with psycho-analysts peering into his mighty cranium. Dr Wilhelm Stekel (*Nietzsche und Wagner: eine sexualpsychologische Studie des Freundschaftsgefühles und des Freundschaftsverrates* ['Nietzsche and Wagner: a psycho-sexual study of their feelings of friendship and the betrayal thereof'], 1917) believes that the philosopher in fact coveted the Master and that he did so behind Cosima's back. His violent rejection of Wagner, says Stekel, is therefore pure affectation, just as his crusade against Christ was always pure affectation. 'Christ was his hero, not Dionysus. Has one ever seen a Dionysus who was a vegetarian, who did not drink and who avoided women?'

The more Wagner ranted against the Jews, the more Nietzsche went on about the Germans, whom he described as 'canaille' ('rabble'), with their 'mendacious racial swindles'. Finally came the two great polemical essays from Nietzsche's last creative year (1888), hurled posthumously in the composer's direction, Wagner having died in 1883. These were *Der Fall Wagner* ('The Case of Wagner') and *Nietzsche contra Wagner*. Tremblingly, the intimates of the Wahnfried circle took note of Nietzsche's fearful truths about the artist who had degenerated from having been the 'German Prometheus' to one who was 'the ventriloquist's puppet of God'. In *Der Fall Wagner* he wrote:

What would Goethe have thought about Wagner?
Goethe once asked himself what the danger was

which threatened all the Romantics: the Romantics' fate? His answer was: 'to choke through constantly re-chewing the same moral and religious absurdities'. . . . Is Wagner a human being at all? Is he not rather a sickness? Everything he touches he makes sick—*he has made music sick* . . . clouds of incense billow around him . . . I feel like opening the windows for a while. Air! More air! . . . How closely related Wagner must be to the whole of European *décadence* for them not to have recognized him as *décadent*! . . . Wagner's art is sick. The problems which he puts on the stage—nothing but the problems of hysterical types—the convulsiveness of his moods, his over-excited sensibilities, his sense of taste which demanded increasingly spicy dishes, his instability which he disguised as principles and not least his choice of heroes and heroines, whom he regarded as physiological types (—a gallery of sick individuals!): taken together it represents a picture of sickness which leaves one in no doubt. *Wagner est une névrose* . . . The Overture to the Flying Dutchman is much ado about nothing; the Lohengrin Prelude was the first insidious but all too successful example of the way in which music can hypnotize . . . You do not know who Wagner is: a very great actor! . . . The most elementary means *suffice*—sound, movement, colour, in short the sensuality of music. Wagner never calculates as a musician, on the basis of some musical conscience: he wants effects, he wants nothing but effects . . . Wagner's supporters pay dearly for their dependence. I have observed young men who were exposed for some time to his infection. The first relatively harmless effect is the corruption of their sense of taste. Wagner has the effect of a continuous use of alcohol. He dulls the senses, congests the stomach . . . Ah, the old robber. He robs us of our young men, he even robs us of our women and drags them away to his cave ... Ah, the old Minotaur! What has he not cost us already!

In *Nietzsche contra Wagner* he wrote:

In the theatre one becomes mob, herd, woman, Pharisee, voting animal, patron, idiot—*Wagnerian*: even the most personal conscience succumbs to the levelling spell of the great multitude.

But even so: 'I name Wagner as the great benefactor of my life,' Nietzsche wrote in October 1888, two months before his mental breakdown. One of the three deranged notes which he posted in Turin in January 1889 was addressed to Wagner's widow: 'To my beloved Princess Ariadne. It is pure prejudice which supposes me to be a human being. But I have often lived among men and know everything that men can experience, from the lowest to the highest. Among the Indians I was Buddha and in Greece I was Dionysus—Alexander and Caesar are my incarnations, as well as Lord Bacon, the Shakespeare-poet. Finally I was also Voltaire and Napoleon, perhaps Richard Wagner as well ... But this time I come as the victorious Dionysus who will turn the earth into a festival ... Not that I have much time ... The heavens rejoice that I am here ... I have also hung on the Cross ...'

The report drawn up in the psychiatric clinic on Nietzsche's anamnesis also makes mention of singing, shouting, capering and delusions of grandeur, a longing for 'girls' and an excessive preoccupation with Wagner's music, in addition to the fanciful notion that it was 'my wife Cosima Wagner' who had had him placed in the institution. He spent the last years of his life with his mother and his sister. He was blind and deaf to all that went on around him. Only when someone mentioned the name of Wagner did he appear to respond. He would then raise his tormented head and murmur, 'I loved him deeply'.

The dramatic way in which Wagner and Nietzsche broke off with each other may be numbered among the most famous stories in the whole of our cultural history. It appears in practically every serious and not-so-serious study both of the composer and of the philosopher. The story, however, is apocryphal from beginning to end. It was on the evening of Thursday 2 November 1876 (so runs Robert Gutman's account, and so, too, it appears in John Chancellor's 'classic study' and in Dietrich Fischer-Dieskau's book on Wagner and Nietzsche) that the two men went on their last walk together. It was at Sorrento in Italy. They basked in the gentle autumnal light. An 'Evening mood!', Wagner called out, cheerfully. Then he began suddenly to speak of *Parsifal*, which signified such a profound religious experience for Wagner the one-time free-thinker. Nietzsche listened in a state of shock. Wagner had once been the German Prometheus for him. Now the composer had become a religious fanatic and prostrated himself before the Cross. 'Why are you so silent, best of friends?' Wagner had asked. Nietzsche excused himself with an appeal to the pitiful state of his health and disappeared into the rapidly falling dusk. 'The two men never saw each other again' (Dietrich Fischer-Dieskau).

This oft-repeated tale emanates from Elisabeth Nietzsche's collection of fairy tales, as is now evident not only from Cosima's Diaries but also from Nietzsche's correspondence. The Diaries indicate that Wagner and Nietzsche were on the best of terms in Sorrento, while Nietzsche's correspondence shows, through his letters, that he had not a single reason to be shocked by Wagner's alleged capitulation to Christianity. Cosima Wagner writes: 'Thursday the 2nd [November 1876] All Souls. Beautiful weather once again, we go on a beautiful walk and spend the evening with our friends Malwida and Prof. Nietzsche.' Nietzsche, in a letter of 10 October 1877, in other words a

54

year after the supposed confrontation with Wagner over *Parsifal*, says: 'The splendid promise of Parcival may console us where we need consolation.'

But what do we read in Richard Graf Du Moulin Eckart's biography of Cosima Wagner? It is *impossible* that Nietzsche should have been disagreeably surprised by Wagner's sudden show of piety in Sorrento. The prose draft of the work had been read to him a whole *seven* years previously during the Christmas of 1869. Du Moulin Eckart knew this thanks to Cosima's Diaries which he had been allowed discreetly to consult for the purposes of his biography. Wagner declaimed the text and Nietzsche listened in silence – 'and she simply noted that it left "a deep impression"'.

Ever since 1929, the year in which Du Moulin Eckart's biography first appeared, we have thus been in a position to know that the Sorrento saga cannot be true. But now that Cosima's Diaries are within the reach of every one of us and we can all consult the original text, it becomes clear that what we are dealing with here is an apocryphal account of an apocryphal account. The reading of *Parsifal* appears to have made not so much 'a deep impression' as 'yet *another* deep impression' – in other words, on Cosima Wagner, not on Prof. Nietzsche, for whom the previous evening's performance had been his first confrontation with the work. This is another of those minor distortions which induce us, even today, to proceed with caution when dealing with the enormously thick biographies in their splendid leather bindings which have been initiated over the years by the intimates of Wahnfried.

8

A Jew-hater worshipped by Jews

There was an important factor which came increasingly to trouble the relationship between Nietzsche, on the one hand, and Cosima and Wagner, on the other, and that was their incessant abuse of the Jews. The philosopher complained bitterly about 'the accursed anti-Semitism' which cast its shadow over his whole existence. 'It has led to the fact that Richard Wagner and I have become enemies and it is the reason for the radical break between me and my sister, etc., etc., etc. Oh oh!'

Wagner had let it be known publicly in August 1850 in his essay on 'Judaism in Music' what his thoughts were on the Jewish question. According to Martin Gregor-Dellin, these are 'twenty pages of the most chilling prose, like the poison which is sweated out after an illness'. This is an odd way of formulating it, in as much as Wagner–contrary to Gregor-Dellin's suggestion–was certainly not cured of his illness following the publication of the treatise. On the contrary, right up until his death, he did not write a single essay nor engage in a single conversation in which there was not at least one tirade of abuse directed against the Jews.

The Jews, Wagner thought, were to blame for everything, for industrialization, for modern civilization in general, for the corrupt world of banking and the press, as well as for the fact that his *Tannhäuser* had been howled down in Paris. The Jew, he said, is incapable of artistic work. He is unsuited to the acting profession because of his repellent physiognomy ('We involuntarily wish to have nothing to do with anyone of such an appearance'). He cannot write poetry either ('He speaks all the time like a foreigner'). He is deficient above all in the realm of music, especially in the realm of vocal music. The Jewish feeling for music has been distorted by synagogue worship, which is the only cultural spring from which the Jew can draw. 'Who is not seized by feelings of the deepest repugnance, mixed with those of horror and ridicule, when he listens to such gurgling, yodelling and prattling which confuses our senses and our mind?'

Wagner did not grow milder with the passing years. In his essay on *Heldenthum und Christenthum* he was quite serious in describing the Jews as 'former cannibals', which at least attested to a fragmentary knowledge of Mosaic Law as it relates to food. He engaged in a dispute with Dean Dittmar of Bayreuth, who was evidently a supporter of mixed marriages. 'That would mean the end of us Germans,' Wagner protested; 'blond German blood is not powerful enough to withstand this "salt solution"; after all, we can see how the Normans and Franks have turned into Frenchmen, and Jewish blood is much more corrosive than Romance blood' (7 April 1873).

He was indisputably one of the leading anti-Semites of his day. And yet he was an anti-Semite who was made much of by Jews, or at least by a considerable number of them. The Jews in his own immediate surroundings were so much his pillar and support that he used to refer to them in a light-hearted way as 'our home-grown Israelites'. Another entry in Cosima's Diaries: 'When we are on our own again together, R. and I speak of the remarkable fascination which he exercises on individual Jews; he remarks that Wahnfried seems to be turning into a synagogue.'

Like so many of his philosophical ideas, Wagner's hatred of the Jews is for the most part pure theory. When brought face to face with the reality, he was as flexible as anything. Are musical Jews really not capable of anything other than synagogue gurgling? As soon as anyone of such outstanding musical talent as the young Karl Tausig announced himself, Wagner forgot everything that he had previously maintained and towards his visitor he was pleasantness, mildness and paternalism itself. He received a painful letter from the young Russian Joseph Rubinstein: 'I am a Jew; this tells you everything.' It was not long before the young émigré became the resident pianist at Wahnfried: the composer himself, after all, played the instrument only well enough to be able to compose a Universal-Genius-Total-Work-of-Art. Hermann Levi, the conductor of *Parsifal*, wrote to his father, the Chief Rabbi, 'He is the best and noblest of men. That his contemporaries misunderstand and libel him is only natural . . .; Goethe also fared no better. But posterity will one day realize that Wagner was as fine a human being as he was an artist, as those standing close to him already know . . . The finest thing that has happened to me in my life has been the opportunity given me to become close to such a man, and I thank God for it daily.'

Admittedly, the limited border traffic between Wagner and his Jewish supporters involved a good deal of masochism on both sides. To begin with, Karl Tausig thought himself *annihilated* by the argumentative force of Wagner's essay on music and Judaism. Joseph Rubinstein was so convinced of the imminent downfall of the Jewish people that he committed suicide following the death of Wagner, who had been his only comfort in life. Hermann Levi, for his part, allowed himself to be carried away by Wagner's anti-Semitism to such an extent that he inevitably began to find 'that the Jews should be exterminated root and branch'. Outside Wahnfried, too, Wagner was convinced that 'young

58

people and the Jews are behind me'. The young Jewish philosopher Otto Weininger was a prime example of this. He regarded Wagner as second only to Christ and described *Parsifal* as a work which must remain for ever inaccessible to 'the truly orthodox Jew'.

Wagner for his part had a great deal of respect for the impresario Angelo Neumann, who travelled the length and breadth of Europe with his production of the *Ring*, which contributed greatly to the fame of the composer. 'Extremely noteworthy that it had to be a Jew.' It was the Jewish composer and conductor Gustav Mahler who captured Vienna for Wagner with performances of what Arnold Schoenberg called 'unprecedented beauty'. Wagner himself may have announced that the whole of Germany was in the hands of Jewish capitalists but when, in 1865, he received 40,000 thalers from King Ludwig II, the composer was shrewd enough to invest the sum with the Jewish banking firm of Hohenemser in Frankfurt-am-Main.

It looks as though, for the most part, Wagner's hatred of the Jews left the Jews themselves untouched. Eager for emancipation and culture as they were, they identified themselves with Wagner's Teutonic heroes. Jewish women had the word 'Hoitoho!' embossed on their letter-headings. They queued up to call their sons Siegmund and Siegfried, so that these names soon came to be regarded as typically *Jewish*, with the amusing side-effect that *Germanic* Siegmunds and Siegfrieds began to die out as a result.

And while Theodor Herzl was writing his book *Der Judenstaat* ('The Jewish State') in Paris, he would soothe his nerves in the evening by listening to Wagner's music. He explained later that it was Wagner's music which kept him going intellectually during this period. 'It was only on those evenings when there was no Wagner being performed at the Opera that I was assailed by doubts as to the validity of my ideas.' Wagner can thus be seen de facto as one of the

founders of the same state of Israel which continues to ban
his works right up to today.

9

Three contemporaries:
Meyerbeer, Offenbach and Heine

It is not out of the question that Wagner's hatred of the Jews may, in the final analysis, be attributable at least in part to the dislike which he felt towards his long-standing rival, Giacomo Meyerbeer, the 'filou' who was said to have bribed the directors of the Paris Opéra and to have been responsible for the *Tannhäuser* fiasco.

This latter suggestion is simply a paranoid tale, mindlessly taken over from Wagner's autobiography by his biographers Carl Friedrich Glasenapp and Houston Stewart Chamberlain. Meyerbeer's Diary shows us what the composer really thought of the whole affair: 'Today received news of the 1st performance of Tannhäuser, which is said to have been a total fiasco. It appears that the audience literally howled down several passages (in respect of both music and libretto) and even to have whistled ... Such an extraordinary manner of disapproval towards a work which in any case is noteworthy and talented, seems to me to be the work of a cabal and not that of a reasoned judgement.'

Meyerbeer's *Les Huguenots*, *L'Africaine* and *Robert le Diable* were at that time the great show-pieces of the opera repertory. 'Robert is immortal', the critic of the *Dresdner Abendzeitung* wrote in 1841 – his name was Richard Wagner. It was during this period that Wagner sought (and obtained) the protection of his famous fellow-artist. Wagner called Meyerbeer a true 'son of Germany', through whose veins flowed 'pure and chaste German blood'; he was his 'lord and master' who meant 'everything, everything' to the supplicant. 'Here is the head, the heart and the hands of your property: Richard Wagner' (3 May 1840).

His letters to Meyerbeer were of a seldom seen servility. 'You alone can help me ... Terrorism is the only means, and you, my revered self-controller of all notes, are the only man who can wield it' (18 January 1840). 'I shall be a faithful, honest slave–for I freely admit that I have a slavish temperament ... Buy me, my good sir!' (3 May 1840). What is the psychological counterpart of the slave? It is the dictator, a role which Wagner quickly adopted when he no longer had need of the protection of the 'cunning swindler' Meyerbeer.

Wagner showed the same illogical inconsistency in his judgement of Meyerbeer as he showed in everything else throughout the whole of his life. He criticized Jewish greed but he himself was well-known as Europe's most talented and habitual debtor. He inveighed against French *décadence* yet dined according to the principles of Parisian cuisine, having first wallowed at length in a bath of Parisian Milk of Iris, which he had sent to him by his Parisian mistress. In much the same way Wagner condemned Meyerbeer's accursed theatrical effects, while at the same time specializing increasingly in magic gardens and subterranean ballets, to say nothing of having the whole Rhine flowing across the stage.

Wagner is really the last person whom one should expect to reproach his rival for writing operas which were 'a circus full of superficial attractions', according to the Dutch critic Leo Riemens in an extremely witty article of his. A circus? But what are we to think of Wagner's very own high-school rider Brünnhilde on the world's only flying horse? To say nothing of Parsifal, the world champion archer, the Eight Valkyrie Girls, Alberich, the world's smallest conjurer, Titurel the speaking corpse and Beckmesser the stand-up comedian. A circus full of complementary attractions: drinks of forgetfulness and love-potions on sale at the bar, the well-known miniature village of Nibelheim and the unique menagerie in the stables outside, with its choice collection of horses, swans, doves, bears, goats and, of course, the famous, genuine, original, fire-breathing dragon.

The way in which Meyerbeer suffered at the hands of anti-Semites of both sexes emerges from a letter which he wrote to Heinrich Heine: 'Ninety-nine out of every hundred readers are *Reschoim* [Jew-haters]; that is why they have always appreciated *Riches* [hatred of the Jews] and why they will continue to do so, however clumsily it may be administered. What's to be done? No Pommade de Lion, no Griffe d'Ours, not even the baptismal font can make the piece of foreskin grow again that was robbed from us on the 8th day of our lives: and all those who do not bleed to death on the 9th day as a result of the operation, will continue to bleed for the whole of the rest of their lives, and even after they are dead.' As far as Meyerbeer himself was concerned, these painful words were to prove only too accurate. The hostility of Wagner and the Wagnerians has been effective enough to deprive Meyerbeer by and large of his place in cultural history, in spite of all the talent that he owned (Goethe considered him worthy of setting his *Faust* to music).

My own feeling is that Wagner's true artistic adversary was not so much Giacomo Meyerbeer as the light-footed, unpretentious and most unpompous Jacques Offenbach. Unlike his controversial colleague beyond the Rhine, this Daumier of the musical scale, this Groucho Marx of the orchestra pit, this Mozart of the Champs-Elysées was the great artistic and commercial success of Parisian musical life. It was not Teutonic gods but their Greek counterparts that Offenbach put up on stage, where he had them dancing cancans, something which at very least bears witness to a highly developed sense of originality. The public idolized him, although, like Wagner, he was constantly at war with the musical establishment. Just as Wagner's *Rheingold* was described in the press as 'an aquarium of whores', so Offenbach's *La belle Hélène* was similarly regarded as corrupt, 'a work full of a Jew's hatred towards the Greece of marble temples and oleanders'.

In some respects Offenbach must have been a naively impressionable man. On one occasion Eduard Hanslick paid him and his family a visit one Sunday lunchtime and prevailed upon the master of the house to play him a few snatches from his most recent compositions. In his *Gedenk-schriften* ('Memoirs') of 1894, Hanslick describes what happened: 'He played something out of *La grande duchesse de Gerolstein* and it was most amusing listening to him announce before each number: "Next is a duet which is especially jolly, no, the verses which follow contain very little that's new, but then comes the finale and that's a very fine piece." Everything was expressed with the greatest seriousness and the most uninhibited naiveté.'

There was little of this naiveté in evidence on stage, where Offenbach revealed himself as an extremely caustic satirist and caricaturist. His favourite targets were the court, the aristocracy, the military set-up and his gloomy fellow musicians, Giacomo Meyerbeer and Richard Wagner. For all that, he got on well with Meyerbeer and even had a certain respect for his opera *Les Huguenots*. But Wagner and Offenbach–German seriousness set against Gallic wit–were as different as chalk and cheese. They fired barbs at each other, Offenbach from his Villa Orphée, Wagner from the Villa Wahnfried. Offenbach's works, said Wagner, radiate 'the warmth of the dung-heap on which every pig of Europe wallows'. Offenbach for his part retorted that there was no achievement in being learned and tiresome. 'It is a great deal more difficult to write piquant, melodious tunes.'

Offenbach wrote a satire on 'les musiciens de l'avenir', a far from subtle piece set in the Elysian Fields, in which

Wagner was brought face to face with his fellow musicians Weber and Mozart. After Wagner ('Here I am! Here I am!') had explained to the two gentlemen why they were such wretched dilettantes, he attempted to play them an example of his own Music of the Future, a so-called 'tyrolienne de l'avenir'. It lasted only a few bars, after which the composer was chased from the stage by Mozart and his companions.

Wagner, scarcely intimidated, loudly condemned 'the genre of modern, immoral operetta' as popular amusement for 'the *demi-monde*' and he himself later wrote an even less subtle satire on the hunger-torn Paris of the Commune, a satire which contained the following scornful rhyme:

> Oh how pleasant and how sweet
> And how easy on our feet!
> Krak! Krak! Krakerakrak!
> Oh splendid Jack von Offenback!

In spite of this, Offenbach was for the greater part of his life even more famous than Meyerbeer and Wagner put together. The whole of Paris laughed until it cried at the Chief of Staff in *Le grande duchesse de Gerolstein*, General Boum, a blockhead in two-four time, who tickled his nostrils with pistol smoke instead of with snuff. The première of Wagner's *Ring* in 1876 brought a king and two emperors to Bayreuth, but this was nothing compared with all the crowned heads of state who had sat in Offenbach's box at the Opéra in 1869, the year of the Great Exhibition in Paris. They included the king of Prussia, the king of Greece, the king of Belgium, the king of Spain, the king of Württemberg, the two kings of Bavaria, the sultan of Turkey, the king of Portugal, the Prince of Wales, the viceroy of Egypt, the king of Sweden and the queen of Holland. The tsar of all Russia reserved a seat by telegraph and when he arrived in Paris, he first visited the Grand Duchess of Gerolstein and then paid his respects to Emperor Napoleon III.

Like Meyerbeer, Offenbach, too, is nowadays largely forgotten as a composer. He wrote 102 operettas of which only a tiny repertory has survived in spite of some heavenly music, vertiginous possibilities for staging them and their generally masterful libretti. It is high time that somebody wrote a well-argued article explaining that it was not Richard Wagner but Jacques Offenbach who was the real protagonist of the *Gesamtkunstwerk*.

The third Jewish émigré, apart from Meyerbeer and Offenbach, to play an important role in the European capital of culture was Heinrich Heine. The relationship between Wagner and Heine deserves to be described at the very least as remarkable. In Wagner's autobiography, which after all contains enough taunts directed against the Jews, the name of Heine never once appears in a negative context. On the contrary, Wagner praises Heine as a writer from whom he himself had learned to express himself 'in a certain, frivolously elegant manner'. The only negative remark concerning Heine is placed in the mouth of Wagner's father-in-law, Franz Liszt. The latter was drawn into a conversation with Mathilde Wesendonck on the occasion of a party, in the course of which she asked whether Liszt did not agree with her that, in time to come, Heine's name would be inscribed in the Temple of Immortality. 'Yes, with excrement', Liszt replied, a remark which (according to Wagner) 'understandably caused something of a sensation'.

Wagner expressly defended Heine against the 'twopenny-halfpenny critics' who had driven into exile in Paris 'a man of talent who has scarcely his equal in Germany'. Moreover, if one compares the music criticism of Heine and Wagner, it is evident that there is very little difference between them in their judgement of Auber, Halévy, Donizetti, Weber, Mendelssohn and Meyerbeer. The somewhat older Heine had simply got there first and pre-empted Wagner in his disgust at the musical life of Paris, with its concern for showy superficiality. He praised the genial strategy of opera managements who staged productions which were so dazzlingly brilliant that audiences were not disturbed by the second-rate music which accompanied them. Wagner said exactly the same sort of thing, albeit somewhat less elegantly and, wherever possible, backed up by the old familiar anti-Semitic arguments.

There were other areas, too, in which the Jewish poet and the anti-Jewish composer shared common ground. Wagner's inflammatory speech to the *Vaterlandsverein* in Dresden included harsh criticism of the sort of communism which, he believed, would result in every lofty mind and every outstanding talent being reduced to sterility. Heine, too, was torn apart by, on the one hand, his sympathy for the 'demons of truth' and, on the other, his fear of 'the sinister iconoclasts' who, following their accession to power, would smash the marble statues of beauty with their callused hands.

At a time when Wagner's fortunes were at their lowest ebb and he was in debt to half Europe, the composer attempted to explain to one of his compatriots that what appeared to be his immoderate need for luxury ought not to be measured by normal standards. He was, after all, not a man like other men; he had over-sensitive nerves and he yearned for beauty, radiance and light. 'I cannot survive on a miserable organist's job, as your Master Bach did! Is it asking the impossible if I suggest that the little bit of luxury that I can take should be granted me? I who have given pleasure to thousands upon thousands!'

Once again it was Heine who gave weight to his arguments, although the poet was not aware of the fact. No, Heine wrote, he felt no sympathy for sansculottism, however democratic its ideas appeared. 'You demand simple clothes, an irreproachable life-style and simple pleasures; we, on the other hand, demand nectar and ambrosia, purple cloaks, expensive perfumes, sensuality and splendour, the laughter of a thousand nymphs, music and comedies.'

That Wagner was influenced in writing *Der fliegende Holländer* by Heine's *Memoiren des Herrn von Schnabele-wopski* is sufficiently well-known, even if Heine's setting is somewhat more frivolous than Wagner's: 'But she calls out in a loud voice: I was faithful to you until this moment and I know a sure means of remaining faithful unto death. With these words the faithful woman hurls herself into the sea, and the curse upon the Flying Dutchman is lifted; he is saved, and we see the ghostly ship sinking beneath the surface of the waves. The moral of this piece, as far as women are concerned, is that they should beware of marrying a Flying Dutchman; and we men should draw from it the lesson that women at best will be our undoing.'

Just as well-known is the fact that Heine's *Tannhäuser* ballad formed the basis of Wagner's opera of the same name:

'Dear Venus, lovely mistress, in truth
  My soul no longer finds pleasing
These endless kisses and luscious wine,
  I long for something that's teasing.

Too much have we jested, too much have we laugh'd,
  My heart for tears has long panted;
Each rose on my head I fain would see
  By pointed thorns supplanted.'

'Tannhäuser, dear and noble knight,
  You fain would vex and grieve me;
An oath you have sworn a thousand times
  That you would never leave me.

Come, let us into the chamber go,
  To taste of love's rapture and gladness,
And there my fair and lily-white form
  Shall drive away thy sadness.'

'But when I think of the heroes and gods
   Who erst have taken their pleasure
In clasping thy fair and lily-white form
   My anger knows no measure.'

But Heine's influence on Wagner's works is even greater
than either Heine scholars or Wagner specialists are generally inclined to assume. Heine's fragmentary *Elementargeis-
ter* ('Elemental spirits') of 1837 reads like a preliminary
study to the composer's *Der Ring des Nibelungen*. It deals
with the world of German myths and legends, inhabited by
giants and dwarfs, Valkyries, the young Siegfried, elves and
gnomes. These gnomes, who are also called Nibelungs, are
disguised as miners and they dig precious metals and gems
out of shafts sunk in the earth. They wear little caps called
Tarnkappen, with which they can make themselves invisible. Moreover, 'they forge the best swords, but only the
giants known how to wield them'.

The young Wagner imitated Robert Schumann in setting
Heine's ballad *Die zwei Grenadiere* ('The two Grenadiers')
to music. The older Wagner modelled the accursed figure of
Kundry, Parsifal's female counterpart, on Heine's epic
poem *Atta Troll*:

Soft her lips, just like pomegranates,
And her nose a bending lily,
And her members cool and slender,
As the palms of the oasis.

And in truth she was a princess,
Was the queen of far Judaea,
Was the lovely wife of Herod,
Who the Baptist's head demanded.

For this deed of blood she also
Was accurs'd, and as a spectre
With the wild hunt must keep riding,
Even to the day of judgement.

And Heine himself, an expert in putting down anti-Semites—he attacked poor August Graf von Platen when he had dared to speak of him as 'the baptized Heine' in the same merciless way as Wagner had dealt with Meyerbeer—left the writer of *Das Judenthum in der Musik* for his part noticeably to himself. With only one exception, his satirical poem in the *Jungkater-Verein für Poesiemusik* ('Young Tom-Cats' Club for Poetry Music'). The poem purports to be aimed at 'the heavenly tom-cat', Franz Liszt. But it appears from a letter written shortly before Heine's death ('With regard to Wagner, there is talk of a misunderstanding between us. I have not in fact written an essay about him but a poem which forms a fraction of a cycle which will appear in due course in the first part of my Collected Works') that this poetical analysis of 'music without art' was aimed not only at Liszt but also at the latter's son-in-law:

> The philharmonic young cats' club
>   Is now returning to artless
> And primitive music, and naiveté,
>   From modern fashions all heartless.
>
> It seeks in music for poetry,
>   Roulades with the quavers omitted;
> It seeks for poetry, music-void,
>   For voice and instrument fitted.
>
> This is the programme of our cat club,
>   And with these intentions elated
> It holds its first winter concert tonight
>   On the roof, as before I have stated.
>
> It was not till the break of day
>   That an end was put to the party;
> A cook was in consequence brought to bed,
>   Who before had seem'd well and hearty.

(It may be remarked in passing that Heine could not have been further from the mark either in the foregoing assessment of Liszt, or, indeed, in his assessment of Wagner.)

10

The humour of *Die Meistersinger*

The Jews, Wagner knew, have (on top of everything else) no sense of humour, the only exception (once again) being Heinrich Heine, the *daimon familiaris* of oppressed Germany. But Wagner considered himself to be sufficiently endowed with a sense of humour to take time off from his dramas of redemption in order to write an authentic comic opera, *Die Meistersinger von Nürnberg*. He himself derived a good deal of pleasure from it, both while writing the libretto and setting it to music. 'There were times when laughter or tears simply prevented me from working,' he wrote to Mathilde Wesendonck in January 1862. 'I commend to your attention Herr Sixtus Beckmesser.'

According to Martin Gregor-Dellin, *Die Meistersinger von Nürnberg* is based upon 'the richest and wittiest libretto in the whole history of opera'. Well, this is something I'd like to take issue with. As a composer, Wagner has so many remarkable qualities that it seems to me we ought to regard his equally numerous character defects with some leniency. Wagner and the Jewish question, Wagner as anti-vivisectionist—but who still reads these inane writings? On the other hand, Wagner's 'godlike humour' (as Cosima called it) continues to cause me problems.

Nor am I the first. 'God! Nietzsche!' Cosima wrote to Richard Strauss. 'If you had known him ... He never once laughed and never ceased to be amazed at our own sense of humour.' 'Your brother is just like Liszt,' Wagner wrote to

Nietzsche's sister, Elisabeth. 'He, too, simply doesn't appreciate my sense of humour.'

This sense of humour, according to Gregor-Dellin, was 'unique and demonic'. But in all the 900 pages of his biography of Wagner, the examples which he gives of Wagner's sense of humour are few and far between. On one occasion, in the middle of a conversation about the occult, the composer began to tap against the table with his right foot. And on another occasion he stood on his head in the Hotel Sonne. Once, while he was posing for the sculptor Ernst Benedikt Kietz, he distracted the artist by pulling funny faces. During rehearsals for the first production of the *Ring* he placed Siegfried's horn on his head and rammed his chief costume-designer Carl Emil Doepler with it in the abdomen. Or perhaps Gregor-Dellin is thinking of the 'unique, demonic jokes' which Wagner made when it was reported to him that four hundred Jews had been burnt to death during a performance in Vienna of Offenbach's *The Tales of Hoffmann*: 'He said, with his coarse sense of humour, that *all* Jews should be burnt to death during a performance of *Nathan der Weise*.'

Comic opera has certainly never been a speciality of the Germans, with all due respect to the charming attempts of Albert Lortzing and Otto Nicolai. Germans do not go to the theatre to amuse themselves, but in order to be spiritually uplifted. Why should Wagner suddenly succeed with *Die Meistersinger von Nürnberg*, written and composed by a man whom people were little disposed to laugh at, where practically all others before him had failed?

Eduard Hanslick made a similar point on the occasion of the Vienna première of the work: 'Humour, repose and unconstrained cheerfulness are lacking in Wagner.' Hanslick, it is true, was somewhat prejudiced, since Wagner's prime target in the piece, the 'malicious old fool' Sixtus Beckmesser, is an attempt to caricature Hanslick himself.

The latter had earlier incurred Wagner's hatred by criticizing the 'insufferable German', 'lethal monotony' and 'alliterative stuttering' of the composer's music dramas. Hanslick, whom Giuseppe Verdi described as 'il Bismarck della critica musicale', was in fact anything but a malicious old fool. He was an erudite conservative who expressed his views on the strengths and weaknesses of Wagner's artistry in effective, modern prose. Beckmesser bears not the slightest resemblance to him, quite apart from the fact that, in his vindictiveness, the composer fails to explain how it is that the malicious old fool has managed to become town clerk and chief singing instructor in Nuremberg's highly developed class-conscious society.

Wagner has painted him in the blackest colours which he could find on his palette. He is garrulous and vain–a somewhat strange reproach, coming from Wagner of all people. He unlawfully appropriates the Prize Song–an act comparable to Wagner's own misappropriation of his benefactors' wives. In spite of his grey hairs, he has the temerity to sue for the hand of the young and charming Eva–just as Wagner could not keep his hands to himself, even after he had reached a quite advanced age. Such behaviour is nevertheless so unforgivable in Wagner's eyes that he makes Beckmesser lose the musical duel in the third act so resoundingly that one could almost speak of a character assassination accompanied, moreover, by the raucous laughter of the whole of Nuremberg. I have never understood, and shall never be able to understand, what is so funny about all this.

According to Theodor W. Adorno, Wagner's portrait of Beckmesser contains a considerable amount of Wagnerian ideology. Walther von Stolzing, Beckmesser's rival both as a singer and as a lover, quotes *nature* as his instructor. Beckmesser, on the other hand, represents *reflective understanding*. Wagner, who was naturally biased in favour of empty-headed individuals rather than intellectuals, makes absolutely no attempt to be objective. Walther has the whole symphony orchestra at his disposal during his singing of the Prize Song, while Beckmesser has to make do with a few chords on an out-of-tune harp.

No, Herr Kapellmeister, that is hardly fair play!

Wagner's thoughts on democracy are well known: he himself was opposed to it in his socialist years. But there is no means which is not good enough for Wagner in his humiliation of Beckmesser, even something as popularistic as the common herd. It is the crowd which is left to decide which of the two Prize Songs shall be awarded the laurel. The result is a foregone conclusion: *das gesunde Volksempfinden* ('sound, popular feeling') can only roar with inane laughter at the daring harmonies of Beckmesser's contribution, preferring instead his fellow contestant's popular hit, 'Morgentlich leuchtend im rosigen Schein' ('Bathed in the sunlight at dawning of day').

Wagner's Beckmesser is a typical example of artistic overkill. He is the dramatic counterpart to Shakespeare's Shylock, whose greatest sin was that he demanded satisfaction for the insults which he had frequently suffered at the hands of Venice's tradesmen. He is also the second cousin to Mozart's Moor Monostatos, whose only fault is that he is inflamed with love for a young and attractive-looking girl ('Have I, too, not got a heart? Am I not made of flesh and blood?'). Beckmesser, Shylock and Monostatos are the outcasts of classical culture. It may be they are no more astute nor more altruistic than their artistic protagonists, Sachs, Portia and Sarastro, but there is no doubt that they are a good deal more human. Their only friends are the few producers who are capable of colouring the black-and-white portrait in such a way that audiences are moved to feel a modicum of sympathy. Just as must have happened, for example, on the occasion of a performance of *The Merchant of Venice* which Heinrich Heine once attended at Drury Lane, where he sat in the same box as a beautiful and pale English lady who, at the end of the fourth act, called out tearfully, 'The poor man is wronged'.

As far as I know, nothing like this has ever happened at the end of the third act of Wagner's *Die Meistersinger von Nürnberg*, where audiences react at best with applause and at worst (notably in 1924, in the presence of the whole of pre-Fascist Germany) with a chorus of 'Deutschland, Deutschland über alles'. But the same opera reveals a curious phenomenon which is typical of many of Wagner's works. From a dramatic point of view, it is an extremely unsympathetic work, involving a good deal of drivel and in which the unsuccessful vendetta against Hanslick/Beckmesser leaves behind a permanent sense of unease.

The score, on the other hand, is of the greatest beauty and originality. Wolfgang Hildesheimer has already shown us in his portrait of Mozart that a vulgar nose-picker is not *ipso facto* incapable of writing music of genius. Richard Wagner is a further example of this same phenomenon, whereby theory and life, man and art, character and creativity do not necessarily have to be in line with each other.

11

An intrigue against King Ludwig II

If we may believe Richard Graf Du Moulin Eckart, the première of Wagner's *Die Meistersinger von Nürnberg* on 21 June 1868 set the seal on Wagner's definitive triumph over all his many enemies. 'Neither before nor since has the Munich Court Stage witnessed such a wondrous production,' he wrote. 'All those involved in it cheerfully carried out their duties in the spirit of the composer himself and the general public suddenly realized that the argument which had raged in Munich had been about the greatest of German masters and that it was the despised, hated and outlawed Richard Wagner who had composed a more complete and melodious paean to German *Meistergesang* than any other artist had done before him. An enormous sense of enthusiasm ran through the theatre and all were agreed that here was a work of unsurpassable marvellousness. All the official and non-official blackguards who until now had openly opposed the Master were suddenly exposed by this work of art as the despicable, shameless and infamous rogues that they were.'

Wagner himself in the meantime had been driven out of the Bavarian capital by this very same cabal. The events which led up to this point and which took place during the period 1864 to 1866 themselves resemble the libretto of a comic opera which puts Wagner's *Meistersinger* in the shade and which certainly put Wagner's 'godlike humour' to the test. The main roles were played naturally enough by

Wagner and Cosima, as well as Ludwig II and the two singers Malvina and Ludwig Schnorr von Carolsfeld, with Cosima's husband Hans von Bülow in a tragic supporting role.

Wagner had fled from his temporary refuge in Vienna on 23 March 1864, leaving behind him his most recent collection of silk underwear, plus a mountainous pile of unpaid bills. He was desperate. Nobody wanted to have anything more to do with a man who was so bunglingly incompetent and habitually in debt. Certainly not Otto Wesendonck, in spite of all his years of support, however much Wagner assured the husband of his ex-mistress that he would 'not be a nuisance in any way' and that all he asked for was 'board and attendance'. Wesendonck limited his support to an extremely modest monthly allowance on the express condition that the volatile artist should keep away from the couple's living and sleeping quarters.

It is worth pausing to consider what frame of mind Wagner was in. He was now fifty–a man of middle age; an important part of his life's work was complete; his masterpiece, the *Ring*, had ground to a halt and there was little prospect of its ever being performed. Indeed, the only three of his operas which he himself had heard were *Rienzi*, *Tannhäuser* and *Der fliegende Holländer*. He felt himself artistically and financially bankrupt and began seriously to consider ways of putting a demonstrative end to his life– 'Gute Nacht, du falsche Welt' ('Good night, false world').

He arrived in Munich on Wednesday 23 March 1864. There, in a shop window, he came upon the portrait of King Ludwig II, who had been crowned king of Bavaria two weeks previously. The composer wandered dejectedly back to the Hotel Bayrischer Hof. The epitaph which he devised on the way there was a reflection of his mood of deep depression:

Here lies Wagner who never throve,
Tempted no dog from behind the stove,
Earned not the shabbiest star or garter,
Honoured by no Alma Mater.

After travelling aimlessly around for a while, Wagner alighted in Stuttgart, utterly demoralized. And it was there that the cabinet secretary Franz Seraph von Pfistermeister announced himself by means of a visiting card which proclaimed him to be 'le secrétaire aulique de S.M. le Roi de Bavière'. He handed the composer the royal signet ring, together with a portrait of the king, and went on to inform him that the art-loving monarch had resolved to place Wagner under his august and royal protection.

A few days later there ensued a moving scene between the king and the composer. The king instructed Wagner to complete the *Ring*, telling him that he no longer need worry about the material aspects of the undertaking. The composer bowed low, in gratitude, over the hand of the king, adopting a pose which he retained for some length of time. Ludwig, who was a head taller than Wagner, accordingly sank down to his knees and pressed his new friend to his royal bosom, murmuring a vow of eternal fidelity. The exchange of letters between Ludwig and Wagner which developed as a result of this meeting borders on the effusive, even when measured against the excesses of the nineteenth century.

'Beloved! My own one!' the monarch wrote to the composer, following a concert of excerpts from Wagner's works. 'Ah, how fortunate I am! Where am I? ... I have beheld the joys of Valhalla; oh, to Siegfried, to Brünhilde! What glorious radiance around Tristan's corpse! ... heavenly life–to hover towards you! ... Web of delight! ... And there the hero sent by God ... Lohengrin! ... Each year a dove draws close from Heaven ...! Tannhäuser,

78

freed from all earthly bonds. Love redeems the sinner! Oh, it is all-powerful! Up, towards you! My thanks, beloved, my thanks, my thanks! May I see you soon! Unto death' (signed Ludwig, 1 February 1865).

Wagner rose to the occasion. 'Oh, how mean-spirited I am!' he wrote to the king. 'Even in my love for you, my only friend, you constantly fill me with courage! I am nothing without you! It is you who teach me even to love! Indeed! In my innermost being I have always felt–and still do!–that you are high above all feelings of weakness–*you know everything*! Everything has been revealed to you by God! Oh, my king! You are *godlike*!' (signed Richard Wagner, 11 December 1864). The truth of the matter was that Wagner regarded the king as a 'dreamer' and a 'fool', or else a 'cretin'.

The use of terms such as these in their correspondence has for years encouraged writers to suspect that the love between the two bosom friends had a practical, as well as a platonic, side to it. Curt von Westernhagen, a leading figure in Wagnerian scholarship, sets our minds at rest: Wagner, he says, was too obsessed with Cosima at this period to be interested in 'an impure relationship' with the king. Ludwig for his part was too much of an idealist to cultivate 'impure feelings' towards the revered composer.

The beautiful friendship which flourished between the king and the composer came to an abrupt end thanks to a second, much less platonic idyll. A vital role here was played by the conductor Hans von Bülow, Wagner's 'deeply devoted vassal and servant', whose wife Cosima had meanwhile become the composer's latest muse. The whole of Bavaria was soon well in the picture, thanks to the local press, which never tired of talking about the arrogant, subversive, squandering, Protestant, ex-revolutionary viper which the king nourished in his bosom. Ludwig alone knew nothing–or, at least, he refused to believe that his 'adored and angelic friend' could be guilty of *such* things.

The fact that in the meantime Cosima von Bülow herself, in the guise of a sort of high-class secretary, had moved in with her lover, only added to the stream of rumours. In order to put an end to this gossip for good and all, the two of them concocted a plan which even the mild-mannered Martin Gregor-Dellin characterizes as 'a deceitful game utterly without equal'. Wagner informed the king that Cosima was 'having mud hurled at her in the sight of the entire populace', purely and simply because she was the self-sacrificing, consoling and willing helper of the friend of her father, the idol of her husband and the protégé of His Sublime Majesty. For that reason Wagner besought the king to write a royal letter (a rough draft of which he was enclosing herewith), openly denouncing these shameful accusations.

Cosima in turn sent off her own petition, which of course had similarly been drawn up by Wagner; it would have melted a heart of stone:

> I sink to my knees and beg in humility and distress for a letter to my husband, so that we may not be forced to quit this land in contumely and shame–a land in which we have desired to do only good and (if I may be permitted to say so) in which we have indeed done good. But if you openly take a stand, my beloved and noble friend, and if all goes well, then we shall be able to remain and shall build a new life on the ruins of the old, bravely and consoledly, as though nought had ever happened. If not, then we must go from here, reviled and abandoned. My adored friend, you who have entered our lives like some godlike being, do not allow us who are innocent to be hounded from here. Your royal word alone can cleanse our sullied name of all stain. It would

be good if you were to protect us and the people would then understand. I beg you to write your royal letter to my husband. I cannot describe to you how I found my husband! I shall return to him in Zurich tomorrow. From there we shall leave for foreign parts, we know not yet whither. Perhaps we shall leave Germany for good. But if you were to consider writing your gracious letter, then I for my part should seek to persuade my husband to return–if not . . . How can we live in a town in which we are treated as criminals? How can my husband work in a town in which the good name of his wife is dragged through the mire? Sire, I have three children to whom I owe it to hand on, untarnished, the honoured name of their father; for the sake of these children–that they may not one day despise the love which I bear my friend–I beg you, my supreme friend: write the letter! If you fulfil this request, I shall bear all other afflictions with gladness. If it is not possible for you to write such a letter, then my noble husband, whom these events may yet destroy, and I shall leave for some patch of earth where peace and respect are granted the weary and innocent.

The only point in the whole of this letter which was not a lie was the reference to the confused state of Hans von Bülow, caused not because the whisperings of the talkative townsfolk were untrue, but because they were *true*. It is worth reminding ourselves that, even while swearing her innocence, Cosima was already pregnant with Wagner's second child. We also do well to remember the risks to which Wagner was exposing his royal friend, whose behaviour towards him had been entirely honest and fair. But it was inevitable that the truth would come to light sooner or later and that the king's prestige, which had never been particularly high, would be reduced to a minimum. Ludwig of course did as was expected of him by his dearly beloved friend, and shortly afterwards the Bavarian newspapers carried a report on the king's letter. Things went quiet for a time around the much-discussed pair. But the calling into question of the king's public position was regarded at the time as an act of lèse-majesté.

The tables, however, were soon to be turned on Wagner, as he well deserved. The première of *Tristan und Isolde* had taken place on 10 June 1865. King Ludwig had sat in his box, fighting back his tears (for some time afterwards his letters consisted almost exclusively of quotations from the work). Hans von Bülow had stood on the conductor's rostrum, with Ludwig and Malvina Schnorr von Carolsfeld on stage, as Tristan and Isolde respectively. The tenor identified himself to such an extent with his tragic role that he tore whole handfuls of hair out of his head. In the third act he carried on in such a way that three fully grown men were required to restrain him. Scholars are in two minds whether there is any causal connection, but it remains a fact none the less that the sensitive artist died three weeks after the première, heaving a sigh of lamentation, 'Richard, don't you hear me?' For years this was regarded as conclusive proof of the fact that to take part in Wagner's operas involved a serious risk to one's life.

Ludwig's widow, Malvina, was herself not a very well-balanced individual and sought comfort with a friend of hers, the medium Isidore von Reutter. The latter established spiritual contact between the singer and her late husband. The dead man had a twofold message to convey: Malvina was to go to Wagner's house and announce that she had been appointed to replace Cosima as Wagner's support and refuge. Isidore was to turn up at the palace in Munich and give herself out as the king's prospective wife–and Wagner himself was advised in no uncertain terms to write somewhat more singable scores in future.

This message was delivered to the young lovers in person in November 1866 by Malvina and her clairvoyant friend. The interview, one suspects, must have been rather painful. The composer showed the two ladies to the door, as tactfully as possible, but he could not prevent the offended Malvina from going straight to Munich where she revealed all to the king, not least the fact that Cosima von Bülow, the composer's self-sacrificing and willing helper, had in the meantime borne two illegitimate children to the friend of her father, the idol of her husband and the protégé of His Sublime Majesty. The result was that the awful suspicion finally dawned on Ludwig that he had been taken in by the couple. 'Can this sad rumour, which it is impossible for me to believe, really be true after all? In other words, can it really be a question of adultery? Woe betide them if it is!' It had still not reached the point of a break between the king and the composer, but the relationship between Ludwig and his 'Saviour who makes me supremely happy' was never to be the same again.

12

The ideologies of *Parsifal*

Wagner's last, most complicated and most interesting work, the Sacred Stage Festival Play *Parsifal*, is also the most sober and slow-moving opera in the whole history of music. The stage properties are limited to a dead swan, the spear and the grail. The tempo is a consistent andante. There is little or no action, except for a moment when the magician Klingsor hurls the spear at Parsifal's head (and misses).

Apart from being complex, interesting, sober and slow-moving, *Parsifal* is above all *sacred.* The composer wrote to King Ludwig II, appealing to him to issue a decree to the effect that *Parsifal* should not be performed anywhere except in Wagner's own private theatre, and that the work should not be profaned by being given in theatres whose repertory included the operettas of Offenbach. When Cosima once publicly compared *Parsifal* to the Gospels, the Master simply nodded. Arguments have raged for more than a century whether, in consequence of this, there should be applause or not during performances of the work. The swaying hip movements of Klingsor's flower-maidens encouraged one member of the first-night audience to shout out an appreciative *bravo*, which was immediately stifled by angry hissing (in fact it was Wagner himself who expressed his approval in this way). Even today the true Wagnerian regards any form of audible reaction after the first act as fundamentally wrong. He successfully stifles any applause then and helplessly puts up with the inevitable storms of

84

appreciation after the second and third acts. He then goes to The Golden Ox-head and reverently gorges himself on liver dumplings.

There is no other opera over which so many voices have been raised, both for and against it. Carl von Ossietzky condemned the mixture of 'incense and eroticism'. Franz Liszt announced that there was nothing else one could say after this 'wondrous work'. Eduard Hanslick found the music to be like 'baked ice', outwardly ardent but inwardly cold. Otto Weininger called the libretto 'the most profound poetic work in the whole of world-literature'. So profound is it that there have emerged over the years an incalculable number of interpretations of the work. In the course of time, the opera has become the ideological haven of each and everyone. With its baptism, washing of feet and Last Supper, *Parsifal* appears to be an alternative mass. It could be asserted with equal facility that the work is in fact an anti-Christian allegory, whose temple scenes are actually black masses. Nor is there any reason why the opera should not be claimed by pacifist groups on the basis of the line, 'Verrückter Knabe! Wieder Gewalt!' ('Insane boy! Violence again!'). *Parsifal*, moreover, is undoubtedly Schopenhauer set to music—on the face of it, the poet regards the sexual drive as the source of all evil. The work may equally be compared to a treatise glorifying vegetarianism, since the knights of the grail consume only bread and wine in the whole five-and-a-half hours which the opera lasts.

Whatever else it may be, *Parsifal* is an anti-feminist tract—the accursed figure of Kundry crawls around on stage for three entire acts. In the first act she is hysterical, in the second on heat and in the third she reveals a quite appalling degree of servility—'Dienen! Dienen!' ('To serve! To serve!'). The Wagner expert Adolf Hitler had his own particular interpretation. He divined in *Parsifal* the glorification of 'pure, Aryan blood'—a view which has contributed substantially to Wagner's dubious reputation, in as much as such a theory is grist to the mill of present-day anti-Wagnerians.

Thus Robert Gutman's study, *Wagner, the man, his mind, and his music*, referred to earlier, contains what appears to be a scathing analysis of the moral content of the *Bühnen-weihfestspiel*. According to Gutman, the fact that Amfortas bleeds from an apparently incurable wound is the result of his sexual association with the racially impure Kundry. The wound is finally healed by the pure, untainted Parsifal, who managed just in time to avoid Kundry's kiss–'Amfortas! Die Wunde!' ('Amfortas! The wound!'). In this way, Gutman goes on, *Parsifal* must be seen as a symbolical re-enactment of the fall and redemption of Aryan man and hence as a veiled treatise directed against the Jews.

This view has been whole-heartedly endorsed by the most recent crusader against the grail knights, the musicologist Hartmut Zelinksy who, in 1982, pre-empted the centenary celebrations of *Parsifal* by launching a fierce attack on the work in various periodical publications. Zelinsky claims to have found in Cosima's Diaries proof that what Wagner called 'the most Christian of all works of art' is really a musical statement of anti-Semitic, pre-Fascist racial theorizing. It is here, in Cosima's Diaries, that there occurs the following remark of Wagner's, quoted by Cosima: ' "I know what I know and what it involves . . .; it suggests more than it expresses, the content of this work, 'Erlösung dem Erlöser' ['Redemption to the redeemer']"–and we are silent, after he has added, "It's good we're alone together" ' (5 January 1882).

This is certainly an intriguing passage, but what it chiefly proves, in my own opinion, is that *Parsifal* is *not* concerned with anti-Semitism. There is no doubt that many of the composer's views are open to criticism, particularly those that relate to the Jewish question. But we must give Wagner credit for one thing: if he wished to inveigh against the Jews, which he did frequently and with relish, then he did so openly; and if he had felt the need to write an anti-Semitic opera, he would not have hesitated to do so.

In any case, there exists a much more plausible interpretation of *Parsifal*, published in the magazine *Melos* in November 1958 and written by the music critic Antoine Goléa. In spite of all the mystical fluttering of priests' robes, *Parsifal*, according to Goléa, is really a paean to the sexual drive. The most important stage properties, the spear and the grail, symbolize the masculine and feminine principles, respectively. In the increasingly puritanical world of the grail knights, all form of contact with these two symbols of sexuality is seen as increasingly reprehensible. And so, when Amfortas dares to consort with the lascivious Kundry, he loses his spear (i.e. his virility) and is punished for the relationship by suffering a wound which can never stop bleeding. Parsifal, the pure fool who has not yet ventured into this twilight zone between good and evil, returns the spear (i.e. the masculine principle) to the grail (i.e. the feminine principle) and in this way sets the seal on the triumph of sexual union. Enraptured, the knights of the grail intone the words 'Höchsten Heiles Wunder!' ('Miracle of supreme salvation'), the curtain falls and the audience pays homage to a work of art which appears to be about chastity but which in reality preaches a lesson in unchastity.

This is an interpretation of *Parsifal* which well accords with Wagner's own tendency towards the elevated and the mysterious, as well as with his warm interest in the opposite sex. He let nothing stand in his way whenever there was a chance of his adding a new muse to his collection. Was it his intention that the *Bühnenweihfestspiel* should be his final vote of thanks for all that had been so generously granted him throughout his life?

87

Some anti-Wagnerians seem to be just as rabid as many of their opponents. Hartmut Zelinksy, to whom reference has already been made, considers for example that the continuity between Parsifal's *Erlösung* ('Redemption') and Hitler's *Endlösung* ('Final solution') is so self-evident that he seriously suggests that the opera should be banned. Shortly after completing *Parsifal*, Wagner had called his conductor's baton 'the sceptre of the future'. Zelinksy proposes that this baton-cum-sceptre should be 'removed with a gentle but firm hand'.

There is just one minor complication here, which makes us hesitate over the question as to whether this remarkable suggestion deserves our support, and this concerns a point which so frequently causes problems with Wagner, namely the quality of the musical score. Robert Gutman, who is no fool in his criticism of the composer ('Even Hitler was more liberal'), draws attention to the by no means negligible fact that *Parsifal*, whatever Wagner's ulterior motives may have been, 'exhibits the finest grain and subtlest workmanship of Wagner's works, reminding one of the exquisite finish to which Bronzino polished a portrait or Mallarmé a poem'. And Claude Debussy, who himself was a fervent anti-Wagnerian, after hearing *Parsifal*, took off his hat to the composer in the presence of a colleague: 'There is', he wrote, 'no longer any question of Wagner's usual, nerve-racking snorting noises. Nowhere does Wagner's music achieve such transparent beauty as in the Prelude to the third act of *Parsifal*. It contains orchestral sonorities without equal, sounds never before heard, noble and powerful. It is one of the finest monuments in sound ever to have been raised to the everlasting glory of music.'

Parsifal was the 'last card' which Wagner was to play. The first performance took place on 26 July 1882. His plan to conquer the world with half-a-dozen symphonies was frustrated by the heart attack which he suffered on

13 February 1883 as he sat at his desk in the Palazzo Vendramin in Venice, working on a treatise on the feminine element in humanity.

13

Bayreuth at Festival time

It is warm and that makes you thirsty. Fortunately, that is rarely a problem in the Federal State of Bavaria, where beer is drunk by the barrel. There seems to be only one café-restaurant in Wagner's home-town where a rebel spirit holds sway and where it is not Richard Wagner's portrait which they have hanging over the beer-pump, but Franz Schubert's. But I haven't the energy to go looking for it. And so I settle down in the artists' café, *Die Eule*, an obligatory stopping-off place on any Wagnerian pilgrimage. The landlady is said to be the only person in Bayreuth who is allowed to call Wotan by his first name. Her café is very famous, not least because of the rudeness of the waiters— 'After all, even princesses have to fight for a seat here'. During the Festival, the culture-vultures squabble over every square centimetre, while their Bavarian sausages are seasoned with sweat from the armpits of Fafner, Gurnemanz, Woglinde and Flosshilde. Everything is still calm. The walls are covered with photographs of famous interpreters of Wagner, above all from the golden years of 1930 to 1944. The café clock doesn't work. Its hands are permanently set at the hour when the Master died, 3 o'clock in the afternoon.

The artists' café lies in the shadow of the local Evangelical Lutheran Church. When Wagner closed his eyes for the last time in 1883, his widow Cosima let it be known that she wanted the grail scene from *Parsifal* to be celebrated there in his memory. The church authorities politely informed her that such a thing was out of the question. The house of God, the pastor went on, was reserved exclusively for divine worship and for spiritual matters, not for operas. She should apply to the theatre instead.

My appointment with Wolfgang Wagner, the present lord and master of the Green Hill, leaves me enough time to seek refreshment in the gardens at Wahnfried. Through the open windows can be heard the tender strains of Hagen's 'Hoiho! Hoihohoho! Ihr Gibichsmannen!' On a bench by the pond sits a young man with curly hair. Beside him is a woman with a tape-recorder; it looks as though an interview is taking place.

'Did Wagner, as a man of the nineteenth century, really have nothing to do with phenomena such as Fascism and Nazism?' the interviewer asks.

'No,' says the young man, 'although it's undeniable that there are philosophical and programmatical links between the nineteenth century of Wagner and the events of 1933 to 1945. But it's quite a different matter whether or not the works which Wagner wrote have anything to do with it.'

Why then did Hitler feel drawn towards Wagner?

'I believe he found him a great composer,' says the young man. 'Though, to be quite honest, I've had the impression for some time now that the whole of Hitler's mania for Wagner was a bit of an affectation and that he much preferred Tyrolean films and third-rate operettas. But some of his writings show that he certainly had a fair knowledge of Wagner's works. And so I think that Hitler must have been a genuine Wagner-lover. But musical taste is a very personal thing. If I happen to like Wagner's music, that doesn't mean that I agree with everything that Hitler thought.'

Well said, sir! I stroll over to the Festspielhaus. The baritone Hermann Prey is just leaving the stage door. He is

91

singing the part of Beckmesser in *Die Meistersinger*. The booming bass of Bernd Weikl can be heard coming from the porter's lodge. He is singing the part of Beckmesser's tormentor Hans Sachs.

The rehearsal has yet to begin and so Wolfgang Wagner has, he says, all the time in the world. He is the oldest surviving member of the clan, albeit 106 years younger than his grandfather.

'There are actually people,' he says, 'who are so naive as to ask me whether I ever knew my grandfather. They simply cannot believe that I really am Wagner's grandson; they are totally convinced that they are face to face with his great-grandson or his great-great-grandson.'

I tell him how much I've been struck by the fact that the shops in Bayreuth have so little Wagnerian kitsch in their windows, whether it be Parsifal pralines or Rheingold liver dumplings.

'That's because of the mentality of Wagnerian audiences,' says Wolfgang Wagner. 'They come here primarily for the sake of art. But in view of the increasing commercialization of life, I can only hope that it'll remain so in the future.'

Is it not high time that Bayreuth allowed a *woman* access to Bayreuth? A producer such as Pina Bausch, for example, or somebody like Ariana Mnouchkine?

'I'd have nothing against it in principle,' says Wolfgang, 'but it sounds a lot easier than it is in practice. You mustn't forget that Wagner's works are governed by special laws. His Kundry and his Elisabeth are, for their time, progressive, emancipated beings. I personally doubt whether a woman is capable of feeling this. It requires a great deal of background knowledge. But as soon as a competent woman offers to produce one of these works, she'll certainly be heartily welcome. Why not?'

But, with all due respect, does he not after all these decades occasionally feel sick to the back teeth of all his grandfather's works? In other words, does he not sometimes yearn to produce *Falstaff*, *Don Giovanni*, *Fidelio* or even *Die Fledermaus*?

'I should certainly like to do so,' Wolfgang says, 'but the answer is simple: I have no time. Don't forget that I'm responsible not just for the artistic management of the Festival, but also for the administrative control.'

And after he has retired? Would it not be a pleasant gesture on his part to breathe new life into, say, *Les Huguenots*, the chief work by Giacomo Meyerbeer, who had earlier been so shabbily treated?

'It's already been suggested to me,' says Wolfgang Wagner, overcoming his abhorrence, 'in order, so to speak, to make up for the youthful misdeeds which my grandfather committed against Meyerbeer. No, the chances of my ever undertaking anything like that are not very great. You can't expect me to produce a work for which I myself have precious little affinity.'

14

The Bayreuth bark
of Cosima Wagner

Scored for full orchestra, the obituary notice for those February days of 1883 ran as follows:

> And so the thirteenth of February came. On this day Wagner ordered his usual gondola to be waiting for him for his afternoon outing at four o'clock. But before that, at about two o'clock, something horrible happened: amidst thunder and lightning, just as had once been the case with Beethoven, Wagner departed this life. Death did not come as a friend or as a redeemer, no, it came as an assassin and as a ferocious thug who attacked his victim from behind. The death-agony was long and terrible. 'Richard Wagner is dead!' Thousands of telegrams carried this message across the whole of the earth's surface and in Germany the sounds of lamentation echoed throughout the nation and through every cognisant German heart. The German nation had lost one of its greatest sons and the world had lost a genius. Half distracted by grief, his poor wife cut off her beautiful, long, blonde hair, which Wagner had so admired, and placed it beneath the dead man's head, so that he might rest more peacefully (Ferdinand Pfohl, *Richard Wagner, sein Leben und Schaffen*, 1910).

This book dates from the period when the Bayreuth Centre for the Falsification of Wagner's Memory was working overtime, for once again the facts of the matter were strikingly different from what we have been led to believe.

In Richard Graf Du Moulin Eckart's biography of Cosima Wagner there is an intriguing passage about the complications which were caused by an 'indiscreet announcement' on the part of Dr Friedrich Keppler, who had been treating the dead man in Venice. This indiscretion threatened to find its way into the papers, it appears from a letter written by Adolf von Gross, the chief treasurer at Wahnfried and the children's guardian now that Wagner was dead. The only person who could prevent the scandal from breaking, Gross wrote to Keppler, was Keppler himself. 'Mrs Wagner and the children are anxious that such things should not appear in print. If you have made a note of your observations, I would ask you to send them to me under seal. I, as the children's guardian, shall ensure that what has been entrusted to me will be handed over to Siegfried on the day he comes of age.'

Unfortunately, Cosima's Diaries break off on 12 February 1883. The true course of events on that fateful thirteenth of February, however, is known to us thanks to a second indiscretion, committed this time by Isolde, about whom writers are still unsure as to whether she is the last daughter of Cosima's marriage with Hans von Bülow, or the first daughter of her liaison with Richard Wagner. Garrulous by nature, Isolde points to a second possibility. She reports a violent disagreement in the family circle over the announced visit of the singer Carrie Pringle, one of the sweetly smelling flower-maidens in whom Wagner had shown such great interest both before and during the première of *Parsifal*. Contrary to her usual custom, Cosima had to raise her voice and the composer retired to his study, in a state of some agitation. A short time afterwards, a servant heard him groaning and asking for 'my wife and the doctor'. Cosima

95

rushed upstairs and saw before her the fatal consequences of the argument which had taken place a little while earlier.

Having abandoned her original plan of following her husband into the next world, Cosima resolved to assume responsibility for the running of Wahnfried and the Green Hill. She administered Wagner's estate, says Du Moulin Eckart, with 'a firm, omnipotent and noble hand'. Even more than in Wagner's own day, organized Wagnerianism acquired all the signs of a sect, in which not only the Jews, but journalists and Jesuits as well, had a negative role to play. As a result, there came into existence something which Adorno described as 'a clique held together by grim eroticism and tyrannical fear, with a terrorist loathing of everything and everyone who was not a part of it'.

The sect relied upon a small number of key-figures. The most important artistic adviser was Julius Kniese, a singing teacher and trained anti-Semite. The army of biographers-in-residence was led by the devout Carl Friedrich Glasenapp. Hans von Wolzogen edited the *Bayreuther Blätter*, the house journal of the undertaking. The pseudo-philosopher and racial theorist Houston Stewart Chamberlain became the resident ideologist; he was husband of Wagner's daughter Eva and author of a study on *Die Grundlagen des 19. Jahrhunderts* ('Basic principles of the nineteenth century'). Cosima's own biographer was the aforementioned Richard Graf Du Moulin Eckart, who must have written his book lying flat on his stomach, so cringingly obsequious is its tone.

These people set to work with such alacrity and short-sightedness that negative signs of their zealotry can still be traced right up to the present. 'They did not say what they knew and they did not know what they did,' writes Martin Gregor-Dellin. 'In the eyes of later generations, they did more damage to the picture of Wagner by their general covering-up of the facts (which served only to provoke a later series of exposés) than even his real enemies were capable of causing.' As a result, only indirect speech was ever used in referring to Wagner. The composer's works were canonized as 'our cause', or else 'our Germanic-Christian cause'. Wagnerians, both inside and outside Wahnfried, called themselves 'the soldiers of Bayreuth's idealism', naturally under the supreme command of Cosima Wagner who, for her part, relied on 'sub-adjutants' such as the composer-conductor Richard Strauss–'I await your commands with impatience'.

I shall never get a real grasp of Wagner's anti-Semitism, but over the years his hatred of the Jews took on a socio-critical undertone. Wagner's heirs preferred a right-wing anti-Semitism more in keeping with the spirit of the times, and one that characteristically concerned itself with questions of racial biology. Cosima Wagner, in a letter to Ernst zu Hohenlohe-Langenburg: 'The entire danger to which you allude, sire, and which makes me think of the Semitism which is to blame for the improprieties mentioned earlier, was penetratingly sketched for me thirty years ago by Gobineau. At the time I did not understand him. In the meantime, however, a part of that danger has become clear to me as a result of a personal experience. One of my acquaintances married a Japanese woman and the nine children of this happy marriage are *all* Japanese! The German element has been totally absorbed; not a single trace of it remains.'

Just as the true Wagnerian biographer reconstructed the Master's life and works lying flat on his stomach, so the true Wagnerian conductor conducted on his knees. 'It goes without saying,' Felix Mottl wrote to Cosima, 'that I shall place all my powers and abilities at the service of our great cause in Bayreuth. I am entirely at your disposal. I am just as ready to conduct *Tristan* as to see to the opening and closing of the curtains.' Richard Strauss, for his part, assured Cosima: 'I have never wished for anything else, dear madam, than what you yourself consider me most suitable for, as long as it is a question of serving our highly exalted and glorious Bayreuth, whether it be as lampcleaner or orchestral servant.'

This same Richard Strauss developed very quickly into by far the most unsavoury member at court. The way in which, for example, he attempted to undermine the authority of his own colleague, Hermann Levi, who was Cosima's *Parsifal* conductor (and one must give Cosima credit for the fact that she continued to support this Jewish artist over the years), can be described as nothing less than disgraceful. 'Is poor *Parsifal* to remain for ever locked away in this Jewish torture-chamber? Why does this pitiable work have to suffer under Levi's "merits"? Forgive me, I did not want to say anything, but . . .'

From Weimar he let it be known: 'Bayreuth and Jerusalem (and all that is imbued and consumed by the latter's spirit) are diametrical opposites and shall never come into contact with each other.' From Cairo he protested about 'the silly artistic rumblings of Jews and Jewish confederates'. From Luxor he complained about 'these repugnant, stupid, silly, lazy, greasy Arabs'. He took a very broad view of anti-Semitism. The letter which Strauss wrote to Cosima on 3 March 1890 is not just remarkable for the fact that, exceptionally, it contains no anti-Semitic vilifications, but more especially because it gives an indirect answer to the question as to what precisely were the artistic characteristics of Wagnerianism after Wagner's death. The young conductor asked Cosima for precise instructions about *Tannhäuser*, which he was then working on in Weimar:

(1) Act I, scene 2, bars 4–5: should Tannhäuser close his eyes again at the moment that Venus draws him seductively back towards her?

(2) When should Tannhäuser get up? Personally, I thought it should be at the line 'Hör ich sie nie, seh ich sie niemals mehr' ('If I never hear her, if I never see her again').

(3) Is it possible that, following Venus's line, 'Reut es dich so sehr ein Gott zu sein?' ('Do you so much regret being a god?'), Tannhäuser could make a slight, defensive gesture, or does he have to remain motionless throughout Venus's entire scene?

(4) Is it correct that Venus hands him the harp? In the piano score, it simply says 'Tannhäuser grasps the harp'.

(5) When should Tannhäuser throw his harp aside?

Salvation came on 6 March 1890:

(1) Eyes to remain open.

(2) Get up at 1st strophe.

(3) Remain motionless throughout Venus's scene.

(4) Venus hands him the harp.

(5) Harp falls from Tannhäuser's hands at line 'Zieh hin, Wahnsinniger!' ('Away, madman!').

Reading this, we can understand what was so conservative about the stylistic principles of Cosima's followers. As far as the scenery was concerned, nothing–absolutely nothing–could be altered. The way in which the Master had ordained everything during his own life-time was the only proper way and would remain so until the end of time. He had never made a mistake. He had never given wrong instructions. Who could possibly call into doubt the Master's good taste? Every unusual gesture, every deviant head-movement was the result of diabolical machinations on the part of the Jews, journalists and Jesuits. And Cosima Wagner who, as the composer's widow, was herself largely infallible assumed personal responsibility for administering her husband's estates. During rehearsals in the Festspielhaus, she sat veiled in the auditorium and had written instructions passed to the conductor by means of a special messenger.

'Not too fast!'

'Three steps to the left!'

'Too loud!'

And so every creative element disappeared from the way in which Wagner's works were performed after his death. What remained was to serve, to restore, to codify and to ritualize. The stage picture turned to stone. The Rhinegold lay in stagnant water. The 1896 *Ring*, according to the French writer Romain Rolland, was exclusively peopled by frozen statues. 'You get the impression that in Bayreuth nowadays people are afraid of embracing each other. Don't imagine for a moment that Wotan dared touch Brünnhilde with rounded lips. To hell with the lot of them!'

Now that Cosima's followers had transformed the once progressive theatre into an 'art temple for the purification of Aryan blood', they followed this up by doing away with anything as frivolous as *singing*. Wagner's heirs developed a rasping sort of declamation, stately in tempo and solemn in diction. According to the testimony of George Bernard Shaw, good singing was regarded in Bayreuth as an 'effeminate, silly, superficial quality, unsuited to the utterances of primeval heroes'.

'Singing', wrote Cosima Wagner for her part to Felix Mottl, 'is something you can get in Vienna, together with dubious intonation, but such a thing is taboo in Bayreuth.' There, 'the emphasis must be placed on the language'.

This style of delivery has gone down in music history as the infamous 'consonantal spitting', sometimes also described as the 'Bayreuth bark'. Once again the heirs thought they knew better than Wagner himself, who was too much of an artist not to realize that an opera 'without true bel canto' grates on the ear, whether it be a work by Mozart, Rossini, Verdi or Wagner himself.

15

Siegfried Wagner
and the German Nationalists

Cosima Wagner reigned until 1906, when a heart attack forced her to hand over control of the Green Hill to her son Siegfried. Siegfried's father had described him, somewhat sanguinely, as 'the blond Beethoven'. Even *externally* he thought his son and heir resembled his colleague Beethoven. Unfortunately Siegfried rapidly turned into a somewhat pasty-faced bourgeois who, moreover, even as a composer (to put it as politely as possible), never stepped wholly from out of Beethoven's shadow, let alone the shadow of Richard Wagner. Which is not to say that Siegfried Wagner was a bad composer. I know some of his works (a violin concerto, the symphonic poem *Glück*, and the preludes to his operas *Die heilige Linde* and *An allem ist Hütchen schuld*) and for that reason suspect that he would have earned a place for himself in the repertory if he had not found himself in the unfortunate position of being the son of his father.

Siegfried's daughter Friedelind has devoted the whole of her life to her father's works and in 1975 organized a concert performance of his opera *Der Friedensengel* in London. The work was sympathetically received. Significantly, the programme was filled mainly with photographs of his famous father, plus advertisements for recordings of the latter's music dramas.

Siegfried Wagner himself was on the conservative wing of late Romanticism. The works of his adolescent friend

Richard Strauss, himself a late Romantic but one who now and again allowed himself a certain whimsicality within this tendency, went too far for his own liking. They were regarded as quite shameful at Wahnfried. Siegfried dismissed such an opera as *Salome* as 'poison of the worst kind', 'a meal crawling with bacteria' and 'the miserable product of malaria and delirious fantasies'. It was probably not so much Richard II's masterful use of instrumentation which upset the Holy Family as his scenery, which could be just as decadent and sensuous as anything produced by Richard I on a good day.

With regard to the Jewish question, the young Wagner was just as dualistic as his father, the *soi-disant* anti-Semite who numbered Jews among his best friends. Siegfried's vocabulary, too, included a number of remarks about 'the synagogue morass' into which German art was threatening to sink, while at the same time he drew attention to 'Mendelssohn's bent nose'. For all that, he wrote a firm letter in 1921 to a party-member who had suggested that Jews should be banned from Bayreuth: 'We have a great many faithful, honourable and selfless supporters among the Jews, who have given us countless demonstrations of their dedication. Do you really imagine that we should refuse all these people admission to Bayreuth? Are we to drive them away just because they are Jews? Is that humane? Is it Christian? Is it German? No! And if the Jews are prepared to help us, then it is even more to their credit, in view of the way in which my father attacked and insulted them in his writings. They all have reason enough to hate Bayreuth. But, notwithstanding my father's attitude, many of them cherish my father's art with unconcealed affection.'

At the same time, Siegfried himself cherished 'the wonderful Aryan audiences' who in 1924 turned *Die Meistersinger* into a German-Nationalist demonstration

103

against the hated Weimar Republic. In the auditorium were such ultraconservative old campaigners as Paul von Hindenburg and Erich Ludendorff, in addition to the most important representatives of plushness and major industry. They stood for Hans Sachs's diatribe about sacred German art and at the end they all roared the German anthem. In the same year, 1924, Siegfried had paid a visit to a friendly head of state. The scene had been Rome. 'Nothing but will, power, almost brutality. A fanatical look, but without the power of love as is the case with Hitler and Ludendorff. Romans and Teutons. We spoke principally about ancient Rome. He looks a lot like Napoleon. A thoroughbred!'

In the meantime, the budding statesman Adolf Hitler had presented himself at Wahnfried. 'It was this summer that we got to know this delightful man, on the occasion of the "Deutscher Tag",' Siegfried noted, 'and we'll not let him down, even if we end up in prison as a result. In Bayreuth we have never made a secret of our ideas. Jew and Jesuit walk hand-in-hand and seek to destroy what is essentially German. But perhaps this time Satan is playing the wrong card. My wife is fighting for Hitler like a lioness! It's fantastic.'

Siegfried Wagner, meanwhile, not least in order to ensure the preservation of the species, had married the very young Winifred Williams, the English girl who was to play such a dominating role in a subsequent chapter of Bayreuth's turbulent history. She occupies a central position in a breath-taking entry dated 9 May 1926 in the diary of Joseph Goebbels, who at that time was Hitler's flight-adjutant:

> Mrs Wagner called us to table. They should all be like that. And fanatically on our side. We are immediately the best of friends. She pours out her heart. Siegfried is so weak. Bah! He should be ashamed of himself, next to the Master. Siegfried is also at home. Effeminate. Good-natured. Somewhat decadent. A bit of an artist,

but spineless. Does something like that really exist? Shouldn't you, as an artist, have a minimum of middle-class awareness? I like his wife. I'd like to have her as my mistress. She shows me the Master's room. His grand-piano, his portrait, his desk. Everything just as it was. A strange experience. Wagner's *Tannhäuser* was the dominating experience of my youth. I was thirteen at the time. I still think about it. The sound of children making a noise fills the room. Children's laughter, where music was once created. It is just the same: gifts from God. We remain talking for a long time in the corridor. The park. The grave. A young woman who cries because the son is not like the Master.

For years the Bayreuth Festival had been firmly in the hands of the German Nationalists and relatively stuffy conductors such as Karl Elmendorff and Karl Muck. Elmendorff was the *Tristan* specialist. Muck had been conducting *Parsifal* since 1901; the work was still performed in the same sets as in 1882, the year of its première. It was the same production as that 'on which the eyes of the Master had once rested'. As a result Bayreuth slowly began to acquire a somewhat provincial reputation, with all the artistic and economic consequences which that involved. Even Siegfried began to realize that the firm was in a bad way and that what was needed was new blood. Who was the hero who should awaken Brünnhilde with his kiss? Leo Blech? Bruno Walter? Otto Klemperer? But they were all Jews. And Klemperer, moreover, had compromised himself by taking part in a scandalous, dissolutely expressionistic production of *Der fliegende Holländer* in culturally Bolshevik Berlin, where not only had the old familiar whirring spinning-wheels been absent, but the Dutchman had worn oilskins and Senta had appeared with a bright-red wig on her head.

105

And so an invitation was sent out to Arturo Toscanini, who was not a Jew but an Italian. Above all, he was the most famous conductor of the day. Karl Muck, who had been passed over in this way, considered that 'the most German of all Festivals' had been defiled; he was taken to a sanatorium, suffering from a nervous breakdown. He was visited there by Hans von Wolzogen, the editor-in-chief of the *Bayreuther Blätter*. He tried to console the overwrought conductor.

'We need an attraction like Toscanini', Wolzogen said. 'Toscanini is a good Christian . . . and he really does seem to get results. In any case, the Italians belong to the Indo-Germanic race.'

'But I'm a good Indo-German as well,' Muck cried out, mutinously.

Wieland Wagner, who was then an adolescent teenager, remembered Toscanini's trail-blazing interpretation of *Tannhäuser* as a 'new work, freshly polished, cleansed of all kitsch, without operatic sentiment, without any perverse ideas about *Germanness*, but exciting, glowing, psychologically interesting and so rhythmical that the unsuspecting listener found it a great effort to remain calmly in his seat'. Not everyone was as enthusiastic. Toscanini's *Parsifal*, one critic wrote, was definitely too little 'earth-bound'; he also missed 'the Nordic element'. This reproach was made by Richard Walther Darré, who was later to become the National Socialist minister of agriculture and the author of the standard critical work, *The Pig as Criterion of Nordic and Semitic Man*.

It was now 1933. In her memoirs, Friedelind Wagner describes a dramatic performance of Mozart's *Die Zauberflöte* at the Berlin State Opera. The conductor was the Jew Leo Blech. The role of Sarastro was sung by the Jewish bass, Alexander Kipnis. Directly opposite her, in the small

106

proscenium box, sat the Jewish conductor Otto Klemperer. 'When the lights went down and Blech entered the darkened pit, the audience burst out in spontaneous applause such as I had never before experienced in the blasé State Opera. He received ovation after ovation, even before he could raise his baton. At the beginning of Kipnis's great aria, "In diesen heil'gen Hallen", the singer's voice was unsteady, but he quickly recovered and sang with such warmth that the whole house was caught up in it. Mozart served to rebuke the Nazis. The following day I heard that Klemperer had left Germany. Bruno Walter had already gone.'

Bruno Walter's concerts were taken over by Richard Strauss. Who else?

It was at this time, first in Munich, then in Amsterdam, Brussels and Paris, that the writer Thomas Mann delivered his famous speech on 'The Sufferings and Greatness of Richard Wagner'. He drew attention to the fact that Wagner, in spite of certain unmistakably reactionary traits, deserved to be branded a cultural Bolshevik in the Germany of 1933. In the end, Mann said, Wagner was a man of the people, who had fought all his life against power, money, violence and war, a struggle which had ultimately found expression in the dream of his old age: a festival theatre which was intended in principle for a classless society. This address led to a furious Open Letter, in which Mann was accused of having insulted Wagner through 'aestheticizing snobbery'. The letter was signed by a number of eminent personalities from German cultural life, including the composer Hans Pfitzner and the conductor Hans Knappertsbusch. And of course the composer-conductor Richard Strauss. Their initiative led to such a campaign of unbridled hostility towards Mann that the writer, who happened to be abroad at the time, found it safer to remain where he was for as long as the Third Reich might last.

Toscanini, once again invited to conduct at the Bayreuth

Festival, was by now hopping mad. Having seen the way in which his Jewish colleagues had been declared undesirable aliens, he swore that for his part he would avoid Germany 'like the plague', including the hallowed ground around Wahnfried. He tore out his hair in anger at ever having allowed himself to be misled into appearing there. 'Over-enthusiasm is harmful,' he wrote to a female friend on 1 February 1934, 'and as far as Bayreuth is concerned, I have been decidedly over-enthusiastic. I did not realize what was going on in the background. Now the whole world knows ... I myself, fool that I am, included.' That Toscanini's place on the podium on the Green Hill was taken by Richard Strauss will no longer come as any surprise.

Toscanini, on the other hand, set off for what was then Palestine, where he conducted the first concerts of the Israel Philharmonic Orchestra, a body made up exclusively of Jewish refugees. The ensemble included four musicians whom Toscanini knew from Bayreuth.

'It was good there, don't you think?' one of them said.

'Yes, but the air here is noticeably fresher,' the Maestro answered.

The programme included the prelude to the first and third acts of Wagner's *Lohengrin*–a gesture which the present conductors of the orchestra might choose to ignore.

The role which Cosima Wagner played in the 1920s was marginal. In the meantime she had become a very old woman. When she used to rock her grandchildren, Verena, Friedelind, Wieland and Wolfgang to sleep, she would sing them the Rhinemaidens' 'wagalaweia'. Her last letter is dated 2/4 July 1923 and in it she praises Mussolini, 'that statesman of stature'. She then laid down her pen for ever. Now and again her daughters Eva and Daniela would visit their mother in her rooms and make an attempt to engage her in conversation.

'Luther cannot be praised highly enough,' said the widow with the 'catholic eyes'. 'He has saved what is essentially German...'

'I can now retire, I have, I believe, done my bit...'

'I should so like to die...'

'It was your father's birthday today. Where's he buried...?'

'How many children has Fidi got...?'

'I feel as though I'm in Paradise...'

'We are in Bayreuth, aren't we? We must never leave here. Not at any price...!'

'The Jews hate everything about the Germans...'

'Where's my father buried, then...?'

'I don't know why, but I don't like seeing women playing the violin...'

'The German language must be spoken slowly and with dignity...'

'Is Richard Wagner alive...?'

'Yes, Mama,' Daniela answered. 'He is alive.'

'Are there many Protestants in Bayreuth?'

'Mama,' Eva answered, 'it is a Protestant town.'

'Oh, that's nice; I'm glad.'

'Are you going to give a lecture...?'

'Yes, Mama,' said Daniela, 'in Kalmbach, in October.'

'What about...?'

'About Richard Wagner as a Christian.'

'Oh, what a wonderful subject...'

'Do you know where grandfather is...?'

'Mama,' Eva answered, 'he's not alive any more. It's a long time now since his suffering ended; he's resting here in the churchyard.'

All that was said was carefully recorded. In Wahnfried, where people were used to thinking in categories such as infallibility and immortality, even the stammered conversations of the matriarch of the Holy Family, who was now a virtual recluse, deserved to be recorded for posterity.

She died on 1 April 1930. A few months later, on 4 August 1930, the blinds were once again drawn across the windows at Wahnfried. Siegfried Wagner followed his mother to the family grave. The two central figures who would dominate the Green Hill during the following decade were Winifred Wagner and Adolf Hitler.

16

Winifred Wagner
and Bayreuth's moral bankruptcy

As might have been expected, the National Socialists were opposed to all forms of innovation, whether it was 'nigger jazz', which unashamedly appealed to the animal instincts in Germany's young people, or the twelve-tone music invented by the Jewish monopolist principle. In spite of the fact that his ancestry was beyond suspicion, the conductor Erich Kleiber fell into disfavour when, in November 1934, he had the courage to include in one of his concert programmes the atonal 'Lulu Suite' by Alban Berg. A member of the audience shouted out disapprovingly, 'Heil Mozart!'

Like other alleged Jews such as Pietro Mascagni and Willem Mengelberg, Kleiber was held up to ridicule in *Das musikalische Juden-ABC* ('A Musical Dictionary of Jews'), published in 1935 by Christa Maria Rock, who actually went so far as to describe herself as a 'professional anti-Semitic writer'. A second impression of the book appeared on the market in 1936 and was graced by a sort of instinctive analysis of what the writer regarded as 'Jewish music'. One cannot fail to hear an echo here of Wagner's bizarre essay on Judaism in music: 'The perceptive listener will suddenly hear the Jewish, ghetto-like rhythms, the nervosity, the movement between extremes which is impossible to camouflage in music.'

The conductor Wilhelm Furtwängler, who, compared with his opportunistic colleagues, was a model of probity, published an Open Letter to the minister of culture Joseph Goebbels, dated 12 April 1933, in which he spoke out on behalf of artists such as Bruno Walter, Otto Klemperer and Max Reinhardt, who had fallen into disfavour. It was an extremely courageous thing to do, defending the ousted anti-fascists with arguments which had a fascist ring to them. 'It would be acceptable,' Furtwängler wrote, 'if the fight against Judaism were to be directed chiefly against those artists who, themselves uprooted and destructive, are guilty of kitsch, soulless virtuosity, etc. The fight against them and against the mentality which they represent (a mentality which is not unknown to certain Germanic types) cannot be conducted positively and consistently enough. But it is not in the interest of our cultural life that this struggle should be directed against *genuine* artists, as well. The point must be clearly stated that men such as Walter, Klemperer, Reinhardt and others will always deserve a place in the cultural life of Germany.'

The Reich's supreme opportunist was once again Richard Strauss. He had himself elected president of the *Reichsmusikkammer* and replied to a reproachful letter from his Jewish librettist Stefan Zweig, 'Your letter of the 15th June has driven me to distraction. This Jewish obstinacy. It's enough to make you anti-Semitic. This pride towards your own race, this display of solidarity. Who says that I've shown my political colours? Is it because I conducted a concert instead of that swine, Bruno Walter? I did so in the interests of the orchestra. Or is it because I've taken over from that other non-Aryan, Toscanini? But that was in the interests of Bayreuth. It's got nothing to do with politics.' It must be said that, even in old age, Strauss showed a sense of decency in his refusal to trade in Zweig for a non-Jewish librettist, a refusal which cost the composer his honorary post.

A curious body made its debut on the concert platform: the 'National Socialist Reich's Symphony Orchestra', whose members wore brown dinner-jackets designed by the Führer himself. It is unnecessary to add that neither the 'Near-Eastern orientated' Gustav Mahler nor the 'orientally Near-Eastern orientated' Felix Mendelssohn occupied a significant place in the repertory. The Nazis were faced with the difficult task of wiping out all memory of Mendelssohn's most famous composition, his incidental music to Shakespeare's *Midsummer Night's Dream*. And so they enlisted the help of collaborators such as Werner Egk, Hans Pfitzner, Julius Weissmann, Rudolf Wagner-Régeny and Carl Orff; in the event there were more than forty such men. Their miserable hack work would not survive the Third Reich, with the single exception of the works of Carl Orff.

Their cleaning-up operation even extended to George Frederick Handel, who had a number of compositions listed under his name which were inspired by the Old Testament. And so his *Jephtha* was re-worked as *Das Opfer* ('The Victim'), his *Israel in Egypt* became the *Opfersieg von Walstatt* ('The Sacrificial Victory at Walstatt') and his *Judas Maccabäeus* was performed under the title *Wilhelmus von Nassauen* ('William of Nassau').

A certain Ernst Viertel wrote a march entitled 'Heil Adolf Hitler'. Josef Reiter wrote a 'Festgesang an den Führer des deutschen Volkes' ('Festive Hymn to the Leader of the German People'). But it would be a mistake to think that the leading composer of the Third Reich was Richard Wagner. There was no sign of interest in his works on the part of the general public, in spite of all the enthusiasm shown by their superiors. The public preferred popular hits such as 'Regentropfen' ('Raindrops') and 'Du kannst nicht treu sein' ('You cannot be faithful'), of which 36,914 and 32,276 copies, respectively, were sold within eight months. A gramophone record of excerpts from Wagner's

Götterdämmerung sold precisely fourteen copies during the same period.

Wolfgang, Verena, Wieland and Friedelind, the youngest generation of Wagners, initially wanted to have nothing to do with grandpa's music dramas. They called *Tristan* 'a mess' and regarded *Parsifal* as the ultimate in boredom. Wieland and Wolfgang in particular were quickly converted, a conversion in which an influential factor was the arrival on the scene of their new, amusing Uncle Wolf, who used to pop over from Berlin from time to time in order to see them. Friedelind, on the other hand, the most sensitive of the four, moved increasingly over to the other side and shortly before the outbreak of the war went into exile in England. There was no doubt that she was fleeing from a totally corrupt climate, what with Uncle Wolf, whom we've already met, Auntie Eva and Auntie Daniela, who were always away at Uncle Wolf's Nazi meetings, and old Uncle Hans (von Wolzogen), who had once written a puppet-show especially for the children, in which Jan Klaassen beat up a Jew for having made indecent advances towards an Aryan girl.

The whole of the National-Socialist leadership made regular pilgrimages from Berlin to Bayreuth: Goebbels, Ley, Streicher, von Ribbentrop, Bormann, Seyss-Inquart, Hitler and Goering. Hitler the animal-lover and Goering the Master of the Hounds attended a performance of *Parsifal* together. In a moment of thoughtlessness, the pure fool Parsifal kills a swan: 'Du konntest morden, hier, im heil'gen Walde?' ('How could you murder, here, in the sacred forest?'), the grail knight remonstrates with him. Overcome with repentance, the young sinner breaks his bow in two. The Reich's Chancellor turned to the Reich's Master of the Hounds and asked, 'Could you ever again bring yourself to kill such a poor, defenceless animal, after having seen something like that?'

The Festival accountant had in the meantime begun to worry. Foreign audiences, who for many years had been a by no means insignificant economic factor, were increasingly staying away. People were beginning to resent the fact that the life's work of the internationalist Richard Wagner was being exploited for nationalist ends–and worse. As Hans Mayer was later to write, 'One cannot be a supporter of political reactionism and put out propagandist statements about sublime German art, Jewish cultural decline and cultural Bolshevism–and at the same time organize international festivals which also provide space for non-German, non-Aryan visitors who, whatever their degree of cultural Bolshevism, at least had *paid* to attend the Festival.'

More than half a century earlier, on 11 October 1879, Cosima Wagner had reported 'a very good speech' by the court chaplain Adolf Stöcker, one of the leading figures of the anti-Semitic movement in Wilhelminian Germany. His diatribe about the Jewish cancer which was eating into the nation brought the pair back to their old familiar topic of conversation. 'R. is for total expulsion.' They noted, Cosima reported contentedly, that Wagner's essay on Judaism in music appeared to be the beginning of 'this battle'. Indeed, it would be foolish to deny the continuity which links the theoretical works of Wagner, Stöcker, Chamberlain, Rosenberg and Hitler. One cannot of course exclude the possibility that Hitler would have been anti-Semitic even without Wagner, but Bayreuth was evidently the place where 'the sword was forged with which we are fighting today' (Hitler on Wagner).

The memoirs of Hitler's school-friend August Kubizek (*Adolf Hitler, mein Jugendfreund*, 1953) make this point in unequivocal terms: 'From the very first moment when Wagner entered his life, Wagner's genius held him in thrall. With unbelievable tenacity and will-power he immersed

115

himself in his life and works. I'd never experienced anything like it before. He completely identified with Wagner's personality. His heart beat faster as he read everything he could lay his hands on about the Master, whether it was good or bad, adulatory or critical. He was especially interested in biographical works, jottings, letters, diaries and Wagner's Autobiographical Sketch. He penetrated deeper and deeper into Wagner's life. Adolf knew of no greater desire than to go to Bayreuth, the national shrine of the Germans, to see Wahnfried, to linger a moment beside the Master's grave . . . and to attend a performance of the latter's works.' And so Wagner fuelled the anti-Semitism of his disciple and at the same time kindled his enthusiasm for vegetarianism, pan-Germanism, Schopenhauer and especially the theory of an Aryan Christ. The composer was totally convinced that the Son of God 'had not had a drop of Jewish blood in his veins.' Hitler for his part had discovered that Christ was the son of the Greek soldier Pantherus. Wagner gave his memoirs the title *Mein Leben*; Hitler chose *Mein Kampf* as his title. The latter work was written on letter-paper sent to him by Winifred Wagner. Wagner was a failed actor, as the failed musician Friedrich Nietzsche so discerningly observed. They were both posthumously enrolled into the Third Reich by the failed painter and architect Adolf Hitler.

But anyone who supposes that the new patron of the Bayreuth Festival introduced a period of the blackest reactionism could not be further from the truth. At least in an *artistic* context. The opposite was the case. Under the patronage of Hitler and of his *protégée* Winifred Wagner, a more progressive policy was pursued in Bayreuth than had been the case for decades. They blew away the dust which had settled on stage and between them they packed off to a museum the sets of *Parsifal*, which were now fifty years old and which had been declared immortal by orthodox Wagnerians. The new designer of the *Bühnenweihfestspiel* was the Viennese Alfred Roller, a friend of Max Reinhardt and Hugo von Hofmannsthal and, what is more, the man who had once offered a place at the Academy of Art in Vienna to the up-and-coming artist Adolf Hitler. Measured against Bayreuth standards, the new production of *Parsifal* was highly revolutionary in concept and was certainly regarded as such by the traditionalists. They demanded in writing that an end be put to this sort of heresy and that the *Bühnenweihfestspiel* should not be given in any other production except that of the original staging of 1882. Among the signatories were Eva Chamberlain, the daughter of Cosima and Richard, Daniela Thode, the daughter of Cosima and Hans von Bülow, Hans von Wolzogen, the long-standing editor-in-chief of the *Bayreuther Blätter* and, of course, their watchdog Richard Strauss.

We would do well to consider Winifred Wagner's position. It is true that she knew she had the support of the head of the government, but things were none the less far from easy for her. She was young, inexperienced and a woman, British by birth and permanently beset by her two rival sisters-in-law who knew Bayreuth like the back of their hands. She nevertheless defied the opposition and replaced party-members on the conductor's podium with experts such as Wilhelm Furtwängler and Heinz Tietjen, whose staged productions of *Tristan* and *Der fliegende Holländer* marked the first radical break with stage-directions which had become ritualized in the course of time. Many years later, the mayor of Bayreuth, Hans Walter Wild, was to say at Winifred Wagner's funeral: 'The bravery she showed in altering Wagner's scenery, in contrast with the inviolable instructions of Cosima Wagner, was in her day no less courageous than the cultural revolution which her two sons unleashed in the post-war world of opera.'

One may have doubts about the scholarly value of the Richard Wagner Research Institute which she established. Its principle occupation was to document the pure Aryan ancestry of the Master and his wife. The complete, annotated and unexpurgated edition of the correspondence between Wagner and Ludwig II, which she instigated, was certainly a major achievement, and one which bore witness to a certain courage on her part, in as much as it showed the composer in a very poor light, cringing toad-like before his princely patron. The two sisters-in-law, Eva and Daniela, once again shook with rage–and once again to no avail.

Winifred Wagner was undoubtedly deeply committed to the Movement. But she was not a member. She was an emancipated woman in the man's world of the Third Reich, a woman who refused to allow men to smoke in her office and who made them stand during her daily conferences, so as to avoid wasting time on long-winded nonsense. She allowed herself a modest protest by introducing two singers into the chorus of *Götterdämmerung* who looked exactly like Goebbels and Goering. Her action had no repercussions, largely because nobody noticed it.

No, Bayreuth in the 1930s was certainly not a breeding ground for the resistance. But it remains true that during the early years of the Third Reich the Green Hill was safer for Jewish singers than any other German theatre. The leading members of Bayreuth's crack regiment were the Jewish basses Alexander Kipnis, Friedrich Schorr and Emanuel List. They had not been barred from the Green Hill by Siegfried Wagner and his widow attempted to keep them on in Bayreuth. It was of course a losing battle; it was unthinkable that Bayreuth of all places should be spared the process of Aryanization. To its own disadvantage. The majority of those Jewish singers who specialized in Wagnerian roles fled during the mid-1930s to the United States and established a Wagnerian tradition at the Metropolitan

Opera, in New York, a tradition which continues to bear fruit to this day.

There was only one occasion when Winifred Wagner's innovatory enthusiasm led her astray. The writer Zdenko von Kraft mentions a tradition dating back to 1876, whereby musicians were stationed on the balcony of the Festspielhaus to blow fanfares announcing the beginning of each act. In 1938 they were replaced by a gramophone record. 'Fortunately the measure remained in force for only a year. It was an experiment whose impious character was soon recognized. By 1939 live musicians were back again on the balcony.' When the political situation worsened a year later, these musicians were dressed in uniforms of the Waffen-SS; the chronicler forgets to include this last piece of information.

All in all Richard Wagner occupied a curious position in the Third Reich. Superficially he was one of its intellectual founders. The philosopher Georg Lukács, for example, believes that the history of ideas in Germany moves along two paths: the progressive path of Lessing, Goethe, Hölderlin, Büchner and Heine and the conservative path, leading ultimately to Fascism, of Goethe, Schopenhauer, Wagner and Nietzsche. But, in proposing this scheme, Lukács has failed to take account of the fact that the Nazis made use of a completely distorted view of Nietzsche, which involved, for example, suppressing his tirades against Wagner, against anti-Semitism and against Wagner's anti-Semitism; and it is noticeably more difficult to construct links between the Nazis and Wagner as a *musician* than it is between the Nazis and Wagner the *philosopher*. The true, die-hard Nazis were in fact not particularly keen on Wagner. He was, after all, a kind of *intellectual* and with his dark, dynamic appearance he looked anything but the prototype of Germanic man.

Nor did the musical educationalists of National Socialism

119

yet have access to Cosima Wagner's quite invaluable Diaries. Had that indeed been the case, then the composer would have ended up on the same bonfire as Freud and Brecht, Kästner and Marx, Tucholsky and von Ossietzky. How the Germans infuriated him! 'The Germans are bad.' 'It makes me feel ill when I see a man like that with a helmet on his head.' 'Liberality and amiability are foreign to the German.' 'The world and especially "Germania" I find increasingly repugnant.' 'The Germans understand nothing, they are insensitive.' Even his own fellow countrymen, the Saxons, were described by him as 'an accursed race, dirty, rude, lazy and coarse–what do I have in common with them?' Towards the end of his life he read only French. German books made him think of 'an untidy bedroom where you trip up over things every time you take a step'.

Wagner was certainly not a model German and had very little reason for being so. He was an emigrant for a considerable part of his life, and one who was finally allowed to return to his own country only after a great deal of hesitation and mistrust. And the same is true of Wagner's chef d'oeuvre, *Der Ring des Nibelungen*, for all its apparent Teutonism. The tetralogy is virtually all you might want it to be, a classical tragedy revolving around the fate-laden love of Siegmund and Sieglinde, and Siegfried and Brünnhilde, a farce centred around the stand-up comedians Mime and Wotan, a collection of magical and realistic nature tableaux, a soporific effective for sixteen hours, and a Utopian and socialist parable. But one thing it certainly is not, for all its brandishing of spears and waving of Germanic goats' beards: it is not an artistic reflex of the Third Reich. There is no musical, political, historical or dramatic justification for such a claim.

Which of the values cherished by the Third Reich does this work of art represent, then? The postulate of its racial theory? The purity of Aryan blood? Siegfried, outwardly the Teutonic Superman, fails on all fronts. All the Germanic gods around him play an increasingly criminal role as the work progresses and they finally perish in the flames of Valhalla, destroyed by the curse on gold and the arrogance of power. No bearskin can cover up the fact that the moral of the Nazis runs counter to the moral of the *Ring*, and the latter is quite unambiguous: avarice and thirst for power lead to ruin. One forms the impression that the history of Richard Wagner in the Third Reich is just one long misunderstanding, fed by the National-Socialist infantry's fear of displeasing the Wagner-loving Führer of all the Germans.

Heinz Tietjen, in an article written immediately after the war and dealing with 'the truth about Bayreuth', comments: 'It would be overstating the case to say that the "party" was sympathetically disposed towards Wagner. In reality, the party leaders wanted to have nothing to do with Wagner. The party big shots came to Bayreuth only "under orders", and even then very rarely. They all turned out once a year, pretending to be fanatical about Wagner; not in Bayreuth, however, but *after* the Festival, during all the hullabaloo surrounding the Party rallies in Nuremberg, where a performance of *Die Meistersinger* was staged every year and people pretended to be favourably disposed towards Bayreuth. I've never produced an opera there myself but I've heard that the performances were so badly attended that people wearing brown and black uniforms were dragged in from the streets, on a somewhat impromptu basis.'

Following the war, Winifred Wagner spoke in her own defence, in the presence of her allied judges:

> A completely new and unexpected danger threatened us after the Nazis had seized power, since most of their leading figures adopted a negative attitude towards Richard Wagner and

his art. Those who proclaimed the Nordic heroic ideal had nothing in common with the idea of redemption brought about by a woman's self-sacrificing love, because the Superman towards which people were striving served the very thing that he himself was keen to overcome by his own efforts. Wagner's works were accused of having an intoxicating effect and the composer was said to have a Near-Eastern racial soul. Even Rosenberg explained in his 'Mythos' that *Tristan* was not a drama about love but a drama about honour; and he felt that the *Ring* needed rewriting. *Parsifal* was regarded by the National Socialists as 'ideologically indefensible'. In the educational centres of the Hitler Youth Movement and the Association of German Girls, there was a deep hostility towards Wagner, and young people used to say, commiseratingly, 'All right, then; let's not begrudge the Führer his perverse obsession with Wagner.' And the Gauleiter who was responsible for the Bayreuth area threatened 'to smoke out the international Wahnfried rabble'. Hitler was aware of these hostile currents and he agreed with me that they posed a definite threat to the Festival. The most effective solution seemed to him to be his annual visit to Bayreuth, which he hoped in the long term would set an example.

In other words, Hitler did not come to Bayreuth in order to claim Wagner for the Nazis, but in order to protect Bayreuth from the Nazis.

I believe that this is true to a considerable extent. And I also believe it to be right that the outside world attached no importance to Winifred Wagner's arguments. It was undoubtedly a good thing that the stale, old production of *Parsifal* was finally revised during the 1930s, but what pleasure could be found in a Festspielhaus where the swastika flag fluttered from the front of the building? Ideologically, this caused Wagner so much harm that even today it remains extremely difficult to convince sensible, art-loving people that it is possible to listen to Loge's Narration in *Das Rheingold* without incurring a share of the responsibility for the gas ovens of Auschwitz-Birkenau. Wagnerians have done everything possible to ruin Wagner for us. However lofty your cultural ideals may be, it is simply not possible to enter into a twelve-year alliance with Adolf Hitler without fundamentally compromising yourself in the process. This was what happened to Winifred Wagner.

She is extremely aggressively spoken to in Bernard Levin's *Conducted Tour* (1981). Levin once saw her in the distance at a concert performance of an opera by her late husband and for a moment considered the idea of sending her a letter, including the sentence: 'Mr Levin presents his compliments to Frau Wagner, and wonders whether she remembers the occasion when she threatened to have her daughter murdered, as the surest means of dissuading her from saying unkind things about that nice Mr Hitler.'

The incident referred to took place in February 1940, shortly after the outbreak of the war. Friedelind Wagner was in Switzerland at the time, waiting for papers which would enable her to travel through to London. She suddenly received a visit from her mother, complaining bitterly about the fact that 'the whole of Berlin' was talking of the disgraceful and dissident behaviour of none other than Richard Wagner's own granddaughter. And Winifred spoke with 'cold hatred' in her eyes: 'I have been sent here to offer you a choice; you don't have to choose immediately, you'll have time to think it over, but you'll have to decide one way or the other. You can return directly to Germany, where you'll be kept in a safe place, under lock and key, for the duration of the war. Or you can remain on neutral ground, on condition that you keep quiet in future. If you refuse, you'll be taken to a safe place. And if all these measures fail to achieve the desired result, then we'll have you annihilated at the first available opportunity; you'll be eradicated.'

'Annihilation' and 'eradication' ('austilgen' and 'ausrotten') were the customary terms used by the butchers who had sent Winifred Wagner to Zurich. Fortunately, Friedelind's travel documents were in the meantime being held by the hotel porter, so that the choice between a German cell and exile in England was not a difficult one to make. While the cannons were speaking, a grotesque incident was taking place on the Green Hill, where Wagner's old ideal was finally being realized: the theatre had been thrown open, free of charge, to men and women from the people. The stage at Bayreuth was now being used for the so-called War Festivals, attended for the most part by audiences made up of the war-wounded. In view of the somewhat unusual circumstances, it was not possible to offer an entire *Ring* and so it was once again *Die Meistersinger von Nürnberg* which served to keep up national morale. There was free admission. Board and lodging was taken care of. It had taken almost seventy-five years but, thanks to Adolf Hitler, Bayreuth was finally democratized.

17

Wieland and Wolfgang Wagner and New Bayreuth

It was on 1 May 1945 that German Radio announced the death of Adolf Hitler. The announcement was followed by a broadcast performance of Siegfried's Funeral March from Wagner's *Götterdämmerung*.

The dead man left an orphan. Wagner's supporters' club had dwindled to minimal proportions, comprising a handful of old Nazis, who had been banned from playing, plus a number of Jews from abroad, hankering after German culture. The occupying authorities understandably ignored the clause in Siegfried Wagner's will which insisted that the Festspielhaus be reserved exclusively for his father's works. To the horror of many, the building was turned into a soldiers' dive and space was made for the *All Girl Show D'Argenta's Fifteen Piece* on the very same boards on which Wotan had once walked. Space was also made for operas which had been deeply despised by the average Wagnerian, works such as *La Traviata* and *Madame Butterfly*, as well as Beethoven's *Fidelio*, the only opera by a genuine and, moreover, an uncompromising revolutionary. The moral of this particular tale (the downfall of a tyranny thanks to the opposition of a single fearless individual) could well have been mulled over in Bayreuth and the surrounding area. But *Tannhäuser*, *Lohengrin* and Hans Sachs were denied access to the Green Hill. The allies did not care much for pomp and ceremony about German honour, German art, German values and German swords. Winifred Wagner looked on from the Fichtelgebirge, having been sentenced by her judges in the meantime to 450 days' hard labour, together with a five-year ban on all active involvement as 'school-teacher, preacher, editor, writer or radio-commentator'.

The question was: what should happen to the Festspielhaus? For better or worse, it was a theatre too bound up with tradition to be condemned to having *La Traviata* performed there for the rest of time. A large number of attractive plans were drawn up. What, for example, would be the reaction in Bayreuth to the idea of converting the Festspielhaus into a theatre reserved only for music by composers who had been persecuted by the Nazis?

The reaction in Bayreuth was thoroughly unfavourable. Pressure began to be applied as early as 1948 by those who wanted Wagner to be given total absolution. The town's Social Democrats fought the local elections that year on the issue that the Wagner family and the Bayreuth Festival were *indissolubly* linked with each other. A letter which was written at this time by a member of the Christian Social Union bears witness to the fact that the spirit of commercialism, in spite of what many Wagnerians might claim, is not an exclusively Jewish monopoly: 'The Bayreuth of today is one of Bavaria's genuine "trump-cards" and, as far as tourism and currency are concerned, it has the same importance as the re-opening of the Passion Plays in Oberammergau ...; but if foreign visitors can be guaranteed the promise of unadulterated productions, rather than anything new-fangled or experimental ..., such potential patrons should in the first instance be encouraged by the thought that Richard Wagner's direct descendants are still working here.'

These direct descendants were the brothers Wolfgang (born 1919) and Wieland (born 1917). Wolfgang had written to his brother as late as 5 April 1947: 'It is in any case perfectly clear to me that our family is no longer in a position to become involved in the Festival.' He apparently allowed himself to be persuaded otherwise; at all events it was not long before he was on his motor-cycle, doing the rounds of potential sponsors, including Beitz, Mercedes, Bahlsen, Siemens and other industrial magnates. The brief interregnum, during which the doors of the Festspielhaus had finally been thrown open to the workers, was now a thing of the past.

But what happened next took everybody by surprise. Totally contrary to the intentions of the Bavarian Tourist Information Office, Wolfgang and Wieland had stepped outside the ranks of the Wagnerians. They purged grandpa's operas of all their pan-Germanic symbolism and warned the traditionalists in no uncertain terms that they had better be on their guard. 'They cling like thick treacle to Wagner's works,' Wieland said; 'they hound young people from the theatre and "successfully" demonstrate Wagner's alleged bad taste.'

The first work which they took in hand, in 1951, was *Parsifal*. There was not a single trace left of the 'impotent pseudo-naturalism' which for years had determined the way Bayreuth looked. Exotic flowers no longer bloomed in Klingsor's magic garden. There was no longer a smell of incense hanging in the wings. The action enfolded on an almost bare stage area. Winifred Wagner sat groaning in her box, obviously having forgotten the extent to which her own *Parsifal* had once been subjected to a thorough springclean. 'And all this is the responsibility of one of Richard Wagner's grandsons,' she whispered.

Shortly after the first performance of the new production, the two brothers gave a press conference on the terrace at Wahnfried, which lay half in ruins. They giggled like schoolboys who had carried out some practical joke. One of the older music critics present ventured to suggest that he found it a pity that it had been so pitch-black on stage. 'Well, I never!' Wieland cried out, exuberantly. 'Do you really want to *see* something as well in Wagner's works?'

Their *Parsifal* remained sober–the staging was not simply a whim on the part of the two brothers. Winifred Wagner wondered what she had done to deserve such degenerate children. 'I had assumed', she said later, 'that it was a question of economy, since there was no money about after 1945. I thought it was a temporary measure. And I was speechless when it all, by way of . . . how shall I put it . . . as a . . . I can't find the right word . . . *fashion*, so to speak.'

Her elder son devised a new creed for the Green Hill, made up of four memorable quotations. The first was by Grandfather Richard himself: 'Kinder, schafft Neues' ('Children, create something new'). The second was by Franz Liszt: 'Der Buchstabe tötet den Geist' ('The letter kills the spirit'). The third was by Gustav Mahler: 'Tradition heisst Schlamperei' ('Tradition means slovenliness'). The fourth was by Wieland himself: 'Mittellinie bedeutet Mittelmass' ('The middle course signifies mediocrity').

Bayreuth only had a right to exist, the brothers knew, if the radical break with the past was permanent. There is something almost touching about the way in which they sought posthumous help from a third party, the much-abused and distrusted psychiatrist and Jewish psychoanalyst Sigmund Freud, a man who throughout his life had unleashed such violent sympathies and antipathies. Working together, the three of them transformed the operas, music dramas and even the *Bühnenweihfestspiel* into scenic, psychoanalytical oratorios. For many years the Bayreuth ideologists had been the anti-Semites Hans von Wolzogen and Houston Stewart Chamberlain. They were now replaced by Ernst Bloch and Theodor W. Adorno, Jews and neo-Marxists, intellectually trained in accordance with the dialectical principles of the Frankfurt School, men who knew all about Wagner and who had an eye for both the positive and the negative aspects of the composer. It was Bloch who as late as 1929 had spoken of Wagner's 'kitsch mentality' and it was Adorno who in 1939 had criticized Wagner for his 'infantilism'. In 1951 they were formally reconciled with the denazified artist and his descendants.

Adorno had once suggested that the Nibelungs Mime and Alberich were anti-Jewish caricatures. Wieland Wagner gave Mime the features of 'an antediluvian Hitler' and Alberich was turned into 'a blood-smeared fascist'. According to the producer, the Nibelheim over which these two characters ruled was to be seen as the world's 'first concentration camp'. In its rejuvenated form Bayreuth was not averse to a certain degree of over-interpretation but such a tendency at least revealed itself as creative, engaging and consistent.

Following *Parsifal*, the remainder of Wagner's output was similarly gone through with a fine-tooth comb. The Valkyries no longer clambered about over elaborate rocky outcrops and Valhalla's destruction was achieved by stylized means and the use of ingenious lighting effects. In *Die Meistersinger* in particular, much of the nationalist sentiment was pared away. For years the picturesque alleys of medieval Nuremberg had symbolized the reactionary nostalgia for an earlier 'ideal world', before the planet had been contaminated by industry, disharmony and a striving for social equality which was not at all pleasing in the sight of God. Now the scenery consisted solely of an acting area in the shape of a clover-leaf, with one stylized tree to the left and another stylized tree to the right.

'The reaction against Wagner's operas', says Robert Gutman, adopting a relativist tone, 'was also, in part, the

129

cyclic revolt of one generation against what its fathers most highly prized.' And grandparents, too, in this case. Wieland Wagner consistently called the founder of the dynasty 'the old man', just as he always referred to the latter's wife as 'Cosima'. He regarded his grandmother as the source of all evil.

One of the striking features of New Bayreuth was the fact that, whatever revolutionary changes may have taken place on stage, the tonal picture largely remained untouched. There were apparently no young, unorthodox Wagnerian conductors, with the result that the first phase of Bayreuth's rebirth was accompanied by experienced, but highly conservative artists such as Clemens Krauss, Joseph Keilberth and Hans Knappertsbusch, whose political behaviour, it must be added, had been far from immaculate. Nor, with all due respect, should the modernity of New Bayreuth be overestimated. There is no doubt that it was a cultural revolution – in stupefied Bayreuth. But what was really on display in the Festspielhaus was a belated variant of what elsewhere in Europe, half a century earlier, had been known as 'neue Sachlichkeit'. 'Everything happens fifty years later in Bayreuth,' Heinrich Heine said, ironically, from out of the grave.

Wieland Wagner, who was undoubtedly the more artistic of the two brothers, acted as the artistic leader of the Festival. Wolfgang Wagner held the purse-strings, although he himself was not lacking in artistic aspirations, with the result that he occasionally took time off from his figures to direct a production. The two brothers worked in apparent harmony but in reality were so different in temperament that for years they communicated with each other exclusively by memo.

This was reflected in the lives of each of their families. Wolfgang's children Eva and Gottfried were not allowed by their mother to go near Uncle Wieland's *Tristan*, produced, she said, like 'an erotic atom bomb'. Wieland for his part created a scene ('Such a thing should simply never be allowed to happen in Bayreuth!') when Wolfgang attempted to reintroduce traditional Germanic touches into his *Ring*. Winifred Wagner, who was officially barred from all further involvement, continued to play a part in this family drama from her position at the back of the stage. She held an informal court in the 'Brown House' which had been set aside for her next to Wahnfried, and she sat there on the terrace in the sight of the whole of Bayreuth, drinking coffee with Emmy Goering, Ilse Hess, Hjalmar Schacht and the British fascist leader Sir Oswald Mosley. Wieland had a wall built down the middle of the garden, since he refused to have anything to do with 'this cabal'.

Following Wieland's sudden death in 1966, the rubber breasts which he had favoured, notably in his sensual staging of *Tannhäuser*, were immediately returned to the stage-store. 'We really must get rid of these round objects,' Wolfgang said. 'My brother must have been some kind of a bosom-fetishist.' Wieland's production of *Parsifal* had remained in the Festival repertory for twenty-three consecutive years, from 1951 until 1973, as a result of which this staging, too, had slowly become due for an overhaul. This took place in 1975. The producer was again Wolfgang Wagner, which resulted in the re-introduction of trees in the first act, a variegated magic garden in the second act and the temple of the holy grail in the third act. 'It is true,' Wolfgang conceded, 'as a producer, I'm not as radical as my brother Wieland.'

But at the same time Wolfgang is too much of a businessman not to realize that the firm cannot make do any longer with traditionalists. That is why producers have been brought in from time to time with instructions to cause a stir by providing a change from the usual picture-books with orchestral accompaniment. It was in 1972 that the then East

131

German producer Götz Friedrich took charge of *Tann-häuser*. Scenically, it is Wagner's most lavish opera and, far more than the other works, it is associated with a number of rituals which have crept in over the years. For example, it has been the tradition for at least a century that at the words 'O Wolfram, der du also sangest' ('Oh Wolfram, you who sang these things') the leading character should hold his clenched fist under the chin of the person thus addressed. And during the entry of the guests into the Hall of Song, it was customary for a widow and two children to bring up the rear of the procession. Friedrich was merciless in putting an end to such infantile ideas. He went even further and replaced the entry of the guests by an apparently parodistic scene in which the refined Bayreuth audience suddenly saw *itself* walking into the entrance hall of the Wartburg: 'Freudig begrüssen wir die edle Halle, wo Kunst und Frieden immer nur verweil' ('Joyfully we greet the noble hall where art and peace may dwell for ever'). The pilgrims no longer wore monks' habits, but appeared instead wearing modern, everyday clothes. One regular visitor to the Green Hill, the politician Franz Josef Strauss, wrote to the newspapers, complaining sarcastically about 'the industrial militia chorus from the workers' commune "Red October" in Leipzig'. Wolfgang Wagner, worried about the firm's good name, decided to intervene. The pilgrims could certainly continue to sing in modern dress, but *behind* the scenes, out of sight of the audience.

The postman none the less groaned under the weight of all the letters of protest, many of which were anonymous, which he had to drag up the Green Hill. Anonymous Writer No. 1 called Wagner 'an idiot exploited by the Bolsheviks', as well as 'a traitor to our German fatherland'. Anonymous Writer No. 2 called 'the red leader of the Festival' 'a propagandist of Soviet ideas'. Anonymous Writer No. 3: 'Shame upon you, Herr Wagner. If he knew what was going on, your grandfather, whom we revere above all other men, would be turning in his grave. I hope that Herr Strauss, who, like me, is an annual visitor to the Festival, will make it unequivocally clear to you in a private discussion what your duties should be as regards the national interest. It has given me particular pleasure to learn that the federal state of Bavaria has announced that if such East German excesses are repeated, your subsidy will be withdrawn. Return along the way you have come, Herr Wagner!'

Wolfgang Wagner did no such thing. On the contrary. The hullabaloo which surrounded the 1972 *Tannhäuser* was nothing compared with the uproar which arose over the 1976 *Ring*, conducted by Pierre Boulez and produced by Patrice Chéreau. A *Ring* intended to add lustre to the centenary celebrations of the most German of all music festivals, and forged by two French innovators–this was a decidedly daring initiative. With hindsight, one has the impression that Wolfgang Wagner was to a certain extent precipitated into making the choice he did. He had initially had his eye on another producer, but the negotiations ran into difficulties at the last minute because of the latter's impossible demand that Franz Josef Strauss should be barred entry to the Festspielhaus. As a result, the artistic and administrative director of the Bayreuth Festival was forced by pressure of time to agree to Pierre Boulez's suggestion that the latter's friend and fellow countryman, Patrice Chéreau, should be invited over on the first available plane.

Winifred Wagner gave her verdict at the dress rehearsal: 'The house has fallen into the hands of a bunch of lunatics.'

The reasons, according to the protests of 'The Action Group for the Preservation of the Works of Richard Wagner', were (1) Wotan, the tragic ruler of the world, was depicted as a violent and unscrupulous capitalist; and (2) Siegfried, the free and pure man, was caricatured as a faithless ruffian, manipulated by others.

The first three evenings of the tetralogy, *Das Rheingold, Die Walküre* and *Siegfried*, were fairly riotous occasions. The fourth evening, which sees the twilight of the gods finally coming to pass, was howled down by storms of protest on the part of the regular patrons. Chéreau was called a 'scatterbrain' and an 'idiot' by turns and silver whistles were again blown, just as they had been at the first performances of *Tannhäuser* in Paris in 1861. The letters page of the local *Nordbayrischer Kurier* grew to Wagnerian proportions. 'Yes,' wrote Dr Maria Teresa Colombo of Buenos Aires, 'it is with a broken heart–and I know that I speak for many others–that we keep on asking ourselves the same question: why *here*? Why did it have to be 1976 of all years? This blasphemous staging must be removed from the repertory, and forthwith!'

The Festival orchestra is assembled every year on an ad hoc basis. In 1976, seventy-three of its members (a majority) let it be known that they were no longer available for the revival of the *Ring* the following year. 'Artistic bankruptcy' was imputed not just to the producer Patrice Chéreau but to the conductor Pierre Boulez as well. Musicians are in general not a very progressive bunch of people and in this sort of situation they have their own way of showing their disapproval. They test the competence of a conductor by smuggling inappropriate passages into the works which they are performing. During Boulez's rehearsals for *Das Rheingold* they played fragments from Max Bruch's Violin Concerto and a fragment from a Bruckner symphony. The evidence was produced: Boulez was no good at his profession!

Once again, the Wagnerians closed ranks. Joachim Bergfeld, the director of the Richard Wagner Memorial in Bayreuth, was guest speaker at a protest meeting on 13 June 1977, organized by the local Rotary Club. One of the questions which he discussed was how far it is morally permissible to blow whistles during a performance of *Der Ring des Nibelungen*. The speaker drew attention to the fact that the flutes in question were of French, rather than German, origin, imported from the other side of the border by Wagnerians who knew what dreadful things they could expect of Chéreau. No, he did not regard the use of a whistle as unfair. How else could the dissatisfied patrons indicate their displeasure? 'All those who are sympathetic to what is on offer can easily applaud for half-an-hour, stamp their feet, rattle their chairs and shout "Bravo". But those of us who have to restrict ourselves to booing are completely hoarse after five minutes of shouting.'

Right up to today the 'Society of Friends of Bayreuth' continues to meet regularly to listen to relatively critical talks not just about Chéreau's sacrilegious view of the *Ring*, but also about the ideological perversities of Harry Kupfer's *Fliegender Holländer* and the hopelessly pessimistic ending of Götz Friedrich's *Lohengrin*. At the end, the speaker turns to the somewhat older gentleman in the third row and says, 'And it is in this context that I am anxious to put the following question to the general administrator of the Festival, to you, my dear Herr Wagner. Do you not share with me and with thousands of others our concern over the fate of Bayreuth, and, if so, what do you intend to do about it?' Fortunately, Wolfgang Wagner is as eloquent a speaker as his grandfather was long-winded.

Now that Wagner has been handed over, within his own four walls, to what the *Richard Wagner-Blätter* called 'the high-handedness of politico-ideological falsifiers', many Wagnerians are desperately looking around for an alternative. Fortunately, such an alternative has been available for a number of years now and is to be found in the extreme north-west of the United States. It is called Seattle and it has set itself the goal of reconstructing Wagner's works in authentic stagings with recognizeable sets. In this production Brünnhilde still sleeps on a genuine lump of natural rock; Siegfried still brings in a real bear (or at least what looks like a real bear) on a leash; and the Valkyries still clump around the stage in full armour. Siegmund and Hunding sit at a genuine table hewn out of oak and slurp their mead from steerhorns. 'The show-piece of the *Ring* is the dragon,' reports the *Richard Wagner-Blätter*. 'It is eleven metres long, almost five metres tall and breathes real flames.'

The opera-house has 3,000 seats; each production is given twice in the course of a season, and news of the quality of the performances has even reached the stand-offish Europeans. When a woman sent in an order for tickets, addressed simply 'Hojotoho Seattle', she received a courteous reply within a matter of weeks, informing her that the seats she required had been reserved for her.

The full address, for all true lovers of Wagner, is Seattle Opera, Pacific Northwest Wagner Festival, P.O. Box 9248, Seattle, W.A. 98109, United States of America. Apart from Siegfried in full armour, the programme also includes an excursion to the Canadian Rockies and a boat trip around Seattle's fiords.

As long as the demand for tickets for the Bayreuth Festival (full address: Festspielhügel, Postfach 2320, 8580 Bayreuth) continues to exceed supply many times over, the American Wagner Festival is not regarded on the Green Hill as a serious threat. The new rival has not yet affected the position of the chief administrator of the Festival in the slightest. Wagner's only surviving grandson continues to be the undisputed head of the family in 1983. Members of the family who have misbehaved in one way or another are barred entry to the Festspielhaus. Not even Wolfgang's own mother Winifred escaped this fate, when she publicly blabbed to the film-maker Hans Jürgen Syberberg about the charming Mr Hitler to whom the Villa Wahnfried continued in principle to extend its open hospitality.

The Holy Family currently includes eleven great-grandchildren, of whom a considerable number lie in wait, hoping for an answer to the question as to who will assume control on Wolfgang's death. They are Daphne, Wolf-Siegfried, Iris, Eva, Gottfried, Winifred, Verena, Wieland, Amely, Manfred and Nike. The last of these obtained her doctorate in 1982 with a thesis on the Viennese satirist Karl Kraus, who once observed that the words 'family bonds' contained an element of truth. Wolfgang's son, Gottfried, and Wieland's son, Wolf-Siegfried, are currently regarded as the most likely candidates to succeed to the Wagnerian inheritance. They are training in the provinces; Gottfried with *Fidelio* in Wuppertal, Wolf-Siegfried with *Parsifal* in Saarbrücken.

One of the stipulations laid down in Siegfried Wagner's will was that three generations, including his own, must pass before works by composers other than Wagner could be performed in the Festspielhaus. That means that Wolfgang's potential successors are stuck with *Lohengrin*, *Tannhäuser* and *Der fliegende Holländer* at least for the remainder of their lives. But *their* children (and no doubt they, too, will be called Eva, Verena, Wieland and Winifred) may finally get their teeth into *Rigoletto*, *Les Huguenots* or *La grande duchesse de Gerolstein*.

18

Bayreuth at Festival time

The town-hall clock chimes quarter-past-two, playing the opening of Mozart's 'Ein Mädchen oder Weibchen'. The performance begins in three-quarters of an hour. Some members of the audience walk up the Green Hill on foot. Others prefer to do things in style and have themselves driven the few hundred yards to the Festspielhaus by taxi, paying for the privilege a sum which, according to Bernard Levin, would have kept Mozart going for a very long time.

Evening dress is preferred though not obligatory. For *Parsifal*, with which the Festival had opened, the women had appeared wearing long flowing robes, but the following evening's performance of *Tristan und Isolde* sees them dressed in gowns which leave so little to the imagination that, if they had been seen like this anywhere else in Bavaria, they would have been charged with indecent exposure. The russet-brown upper parts of the women's bodies betray the fact that they have recently returned from basking on Mediterranean beaches. They are married to today's leaders – men from middle management, thirty-five to forty-five years of age, with elbows like razors. The percentage of Bavarian fat necks is noticeably lower than I had expected and, on closer investigation, it turns out that most of the audience are speaking French.

There is always an extremely friendly atmosphere here. Children play in the gardens around the Festspielhaus, without being chased away by officious attendants in peaked caps. The notice in the cloakroom is not the usual 'No smoking', but a polite request, 'Kindly refrain from smoking'. The press office, the usherettes, the man in the kiosk selling books and records and the girls on the champagne stall are all civility itself. The members of the audience have emerged from the auditorium and are sitting, munching away and genuinely enjoying themselves. During the long intervals there is a general move in the direction of the Festival Restaurant, where visitors mix democratically with the natives. Jointly and in association they all eat their Bavarian sausages.

Wagner had written to King Ludwig II on 1 October 1874, two years before his private theatre was officially opened, explaining how he imagined the formal running of things: 'Every performance begins at 4 o'clock in the afternoon; the second act begins at 6 o'clock and the third act begins at 8, so that there will be a decent interval between each act when the audience will have an opportunity to wander through the theatre gardens and to consume some food, so that at the end, at a signal from the trombones, they may return to their seats feeling completely refreshed.' This is by no means the worst of Wagnerian traditions and it has been honoured ever since. Just like the much-discussed wooden seats, specially designed by the composer to prevent his supporters from dropping off to sleep. At first, the degree of discomfort which these seats cause comes as a pleasant surprise. At a second stage–after about an hour-and-a-half–they begin to fall noticeably short of one's expectations. This stage begins with a slight tendency to shift one's weight from side to side, a tendency which soon passes over into a violent tingling sensation in one's lower limbs. The next stage is reached when the visitor begins to writhe on his seat as though it were sprinkled with itching-powder. Finally all that prevents the inexperienced visitor to Bayreuth from massaging his posterior in public is the sense of false modesty which he feels. The fact that the wood has never been replaced by plush says much for the genuineness of public interest. Audiences really do come because of Wagner and not simply to see the latest stole or so-and-so's latest wife.

There is a remarkable discrepancy between the generally enthusiastic applause at the end of a performance and the gossip that goes on during the intervals. There are a great many complaints, for instance over the staging of *Der fliegende Holländer*, which is orthodox in its setting but daring in its characterization. The leading female figure, Senta, the sea-farer's daughter, is traditionally interpreted as a self-effacing *tragédienne* with blonde plaits. On this occasion she is a pathological visionary who derives hysterical pleasure from being paired off with a total stranger whom her father has brought home with him. Admittedly, she is sufficiently broad-minded not to take exception to the fact that he, the Dutch-man, is as black as ebony. Guess who's coming to dinner!

On the question of *Tristan und Isolde*, it appears that audiences on the whole are not dissatisfied. Except with Isolde's Transfiguration, interpreted as a feverish dream on the part of the dying hero. When the last note has died away and the spotlight glides from Isolde to Tristan, it becomes clear that her presence has been simply a vision: he is seen resting not in the arms of his lover, but in those of his companion Kurwenal. There is a good deal of discussion over the champagne about Wagner's stage-directions, which dictate an alternative ending: 'That is how the Master wanted it and that is how it ought to remain until the end of time' (Wagnerian proverb).

The daily newspapers which are read over the breakfast table in the Hotel Bayrischer Hof are the *Nordbayrische Zeitung* and the supra-regional *Süddeutsche Zeitung*. The latter will no doubt include yet another article by Hartmut

Zelinsky, explaining why *Parsifal* is an anti-Semitic opera. This will be followed by a piece by Joachim Kaiser, the music critic of the *Süddeutsche Zeitung*, telling the readers why this is nonsense. The composer Dieter Schnebel rounds off the discussion by putting forward the theory that there is no such thing as an anti-Semitic opera. 'I myself am a middle-of-the-road Wagner lover,' he says. 'I prefer Verdi. I've heard a lot of Wagner's music and I don't believe that it's made an anti-Semite of me.'

Such a controversial work demands a controversial presentation. The production has once again been entrusted to Götz Friedrich and is greeted by a few cultivated boos on the part of the audience. The producer has overlaid the opera with his usual gloss of social criticism—one part alternative living plus two parts anti-authoritarianism, to-gether with a timely warning about the curse of technology. The grail temple is a quarter crenellated. The grail king Titurel addresses his invalid son Amfortas by means of a video-projected image. The magician Klingsor rules over a world of robots, which receive their instructions via a hand microphone. The flower-maidens, it appears, spend their free time working in Bayreuth's brothels, and their whore-like appearance contrasts somewhat with their sweetly cloy-ing text: 'I am the prettiest . . . I am prettier . . . No, I smell sweeter.' It is now about fifty years since Karl Muck broke off conducting at this point and said, 'Ladies, I'm not in a position to say from down here how you smell, but the ladies on my right have begun to smell a quarter of a bar too soon.'

The press conference which follows the performance is naturally dominated by Wolfgang Wagner. No, he says, he has certainly no intention of entering into a discussion with Mr Zelinsky. 'There is no point in arguing with people who are so pig-headed as to persist in their absurd opinions.' Wolfgang is unlucky to have found himself caught up in the debate which has recently flared up. Questions of race are

still a sensitive issue on the Green Hill, however irreproach-
ably the management may have behaved in this respect in
New, post-war Bayreuth. However many socially critical
productions of *Parsifal* may be staged there, and notwithstanding the presence of a Jewish conductor, a Thai stage-
designer, an Indian chorus-master and at least one black in
the cast-list, the long shadows of Richard and Cosima
Wagner continue to lie over the Festspielhaus.

The black in this particular socially critical production is
Simon Estes, the interpreter of the permanently bleeding
Amfortas. A woman from an American television company
asks him what it feels like to be a black singer, here in
Bayreuth . . . She is not even given a chance to complete her
question. Wolfgang Wagner seizes the microphone angrily,
'I refuse to allow that question! Here in Bayreuth we don't
look at the colour of a man's skin! Our only criterion is the
quality of the interpretation. It may be that questions of race
are a problem elsewhere, but that is certainly not the case
here in Bayreuth!' He then orders the questioner to leave the
room, together with her camera crew and sound engineers.

The black singer looks on somewhat embarrassed, like most
of the others who are present. He says later that he did not find
the question in the least discriminatory. 'I am grateful and glad
that Wolfgang Wagner is colour-blind, but I found his reaction excessive. If I had not been black, I'd have turned red with
substitute shame.' Wolfgang's intervention, following what
had been a perfectly legitimate question, strikes me as somewhat over-emotional. But we should remember that the man
has fallen heir to an unenviable ideological legacy. Grandpa's
racial hatred continues to be a festering wound in Bayreuth's
flesh, and one which will never stop bleeding.

Die Meistersinger von Nürnberg was produced by Wolfgang Wagner himself. It is clear that the weight of the
Wagnerians hangs around his neck like the biblical mill-

stone. They have had to put up with Chéreau's *Ring* for four years but by way of a sop they now receive a production which avoids taking any risks at all. The rustic, half-timbered exteriors have been brought out of cold storage, the apprentices dance their folksy dances, and the Festival Meadow in the closing scene is 'a joy to behold'. 'Cosmopolitan Bayreuth' is suddenly back in the provinces again.

And yet the production has some nice touches. Wolfgang has finally attempted to tackle the problem of Beckmesser. His Beckmesser is no querulous old fool, ripe for pensioning off, but is young, lively and on the make, so that his final humiliation is somewhat less embarrassing than usual. But the price which Wolfgang has to pay for this is the loss of all psychological credibility. He should have known better: his grandfather's questionable sense of humour is not at all easy to realize on stage. The mood of conciliation extends to the point where, five minutes after having been made to look extremely silly and forced to flee, Beckmesser is drawn back into the circle of merry-making Nurembergers; silently, he presses the hand of Hans Sachs, the man who had just humiliated him. But life is not like that. Beckmesser is not a thick-skulled Bavarian who can be made to forget an insult which he has suffered by a couple of good-natured pats on the back; he is an irascible intellectual with a vulnerable sense of self-esteem; he forgets nothing and forgives no one. Instead of this, we see him standing, leaning against the linden-tree, like some crestfallen schoolboy, waiting for the end of the opera.

And so the Festspielhaus in Bayreuth has finally become a comparatively normal opera-house. What it offers is for the most part culinary art, diversified by the occasional experiment. It has a few good producers under contract, as well as examples of the modern type of producer who likes to come between the audience and the work of art in question. For

143

years now audiences have no longer been made up of Nazis disguised in evening dress, but comprise the familiar, everyday bourgeoisie, who are just as conservative as in Vienna, Düsseldorf, Paris or New York. A true Wagnerian tenor or Wagnerian soprano is rare nowadays, even in Bayreuth, but it must be said that the singers here do not sing any *worse* than elsewhere.

There is one thing which appears to be beyond dispute: all that goes on at present on the Green Hill no longer has anything to do with the German Nationalism of Cosima and Siegfried Wagner, let alone the National Socialism of Winifred Wagner and Adolf Hitler. And occasionally it may even have nothing to do with the Wagner of Richard Wagner. The composer might not even recognize his own Festspielhaus any more. In all the one-and-a-half-inch thick pile of printed material which accompanied the new *Parsifal*, I never once came across a reference to the fact that the conductor James Levine ... Be that as it may, the conductor of the *Ring* in the centenary year of 1983 is Sir Georg Solti, another representative of the type whom, in an artistic context, Wagner Senior assumed incapable of anything more than synagogue gurglings. What did his grandson say to this at the press conference? 'It may be that questions of race are a problem elsewhere, but that is certainly not the case here in Bayreuth...'

Really? The role of Wotan in the 1983 *Ring* had been reserved for the same Simon Estes who, a year earlier, had sung a black Amfortas and a black Dutchman. In September 1982 he received a telegram: 'Much regret. Decision negative. Has nothing to do with your voice or musical abilities.' It *was* therefore a question of the colour of his skin. A black Amfortas–why not? A black Dutchman–certainly! But a black Wotan, a black chief of all the Teutonic tribes, is still too much for the new, open, humanized, denazified, deteutonized Bayreuth.

19

A peace-treaty with Richard Wagner

It is more than a hundred years since Wagner closed his eyes for the last time in the Palazzo Vendramin. Yet polemicists wax just as indignant today about his person and his works as they did on the occasion of the twenty-fifth, fiftieth and seventy-fifth anniversaries of his death. What other poet, thinker or composer, apart from Karl Marx and Heinrich Heine, has managed to kick up so much dust after such a length of time? My compliments, Herr Kapellmeister.

'As long as Wagner's operas continue to be performed,' said the novelist Hans Rothe, 'there remains the possibility of a return to some National-Socialist doctrine of salvation.'

'You can't *keep on* blaming Wagner for the fact that he confused the human brain,' said Wieland Wagner. 'The human brain is already confused enough without Richard Wagner.'

'German intellectuals would not have opened their arms quite so readily to Hitler,' says the writer Erich Kuby, 'if they had not been prepared for it by Wagner, Bayreuth and the Wagnerians.'

'The whole of Bayreuth, the whole of Wilhelminian Germany and the whole bourgeois set-up,' said the literary historian Hans Mayer, 'were just as anti-Semitic as Wagner himself, and not just because of Wagner.'

'He used music,' says the music historian Hartmut Zelinsky, 'in a wholly conscious way as a kind of drug, and a kind of narcotic-cum-ideological vehicle.'

'The music of the Nazis is not the Prelude to *Die Meistersinger* but the Horst-Wessel-Lied,' said the philosopher Ernst Bloch. 'They deserve nothing better and no other respect can be paid them.'

There is no doubt that Wagner himself is in part to blame for the fact that after all these years the dust has not yet settled around him. If his life-style had been less outrageous, his claims less extravagant and his theories more temperate, he would have been seen at once as an undisputed artist. Unfortunately, he chose the wrong friends, or rather the wrong friends chose him, as a reactionary symbol which was out of line with his life and work.

One of them, Wilhelm Furtwängler, conducted Wagner's *Die Meistersinger von Nürnberg* on 21 March 1933 in a performance which was held at the express wish of Germany's new head of state, Adolf Hitler, to mark the founding of the Third Reich. It was undoubtedly a political gesture on the part of both Wilhelm Furtwängler and Adolf Hitler. But it was not so on the part of Richard Wagner, whose *Meistersinger*–even after a detailed examination of the libretto–proves to have not a single point in common with the political heresy in question. The Nazis could just as well have chosen Weber's *Der Freischütz* or Mozart's *Die Zauberflöte*, without Weber or Mozart thereby being accused of National-Socialist sympathies *après la lettre*.

Hitler's taste in art is an interesting subject for his biographers, but it can scarcely be said to represent a social norm, either in a negative or in a positive sense. His favourite artist was Carl Spitzweg, the satirical portraitist of the petty bourgeoisie. Does this fact make Spitzweg's paintings any the better or worse? Hitler also liked dogs. Are all dog-lovers therefore Nazis? When Hitler's colleague as a dictator, Joseph Stalin, was found dead in his country dacha, a record of Mozart's Piano Concerto no. 23, K. 488, was found lying on the turntable. But no one would wish to claim as a result of this that Mozart was a harbinger of the Gulag Archipelago. It was performing artists who collaborated with the Nazis, not Wagner himself. They remained behind, working for a regime which hounded Bruno Walter into exile and which toppled the statue of Felix Mendelssohn from its pedestal. In order to stay in office, they legitimized this kind of barbarity and, worse than that, it was thanks to them that the Third Reich acquired for itself a sort of aura of culture.

However, the fact that a certain Adolf Hitler sat in seat 15 of row 24 at the performance of *Die Meistersinger* in question, says nothing about the work itself. The ability of a piece of music to make a political statement is in any case somewhat limited. In the particular case of Wagner it is based on little more than a meagre passage in the libretto: sacred German art in *Die Meistersinger von Nürnberg* and the Eastern hordes in *Lohengrin*. From a social point of view, music is the most impotent of all the muses. It can suggest a great deal; it can serve as an ornament; and it can be progressive or conservative. But there is no specifically Fascist kind of music, just as there is no anti-Fascist chord of a diminished seventh; and, at least as far as I am aware, musicologists have not yet succeeded in identifying a socio-democratic fifth. Admittedly, there exists a certain predilection for three-four time in a totalitarian milieu. When Wagner wanted to please the newly installed Prince Wilhelm I, he promptly composed a martial *Kaisermarsch*. He similarly wrote a *Huldigungsmarsch* for King Ludwig II and a *Grosser Festmarsch* in order to commemorate the centenary of the American War of Independence. From a compositional point of view, all three of them were resounding failures. Nobody speaks of these works any longer and no orchestra still includes them in its repertory.

147

Wagner had many ambitions. He would have liked, for example, to have seen the Jews driven out of what was then Germany. But it was also his ambition in life not only to invent the Music of the Future but to discover a type of specifically anti-Jewish music, an ambition in which he failed miserably. After all, Felix Mendelssohn has not gone down in musical history as a composer of Jewish piano sonatas, Jewish symphonies and Jewish oratorios. On the contrary, his works are just as German, and just as Germanic, as those of Robert Schumann, Johannes Brahms and Richard Wagner. In spite of all the racist Nuremberg Decrees, there is no Fascist or anti-Fascist, Jewish or anti-Jewish way of playing the 'cello, or of running, mountain-climbing, furthering the frontiers of knowledge, acting Ibsen or singing Wagner.

True—the muses are not wholly innocent. A number of them move with equal facility on the heights of Olympus as they do in brothels. Albert Speer's arena in Nuremberg for the party conferences of the Third Reich was not an example of progressive architecture. In 1942, at the Vienna Burgtheater, the actor Werner Kraus portrayed the character of Shylock in such a pointedly anti-Semitic fashion that the audience was brought to fever pitch and accompanied almost every line with clapping and stamping of feet. In the gardens of the Festspielhaus at Bayreuth there is a bust of Wagner by Hitler's favourite sculptor, Arno Breker. It depicts the composer as a totalitarian dictator with protruding eyes and a sharply projecting jaw, certainly not as a man plagued by doubt and tormented by troubled dreams, who knew that Mendelssohn could modulate better than he could.

But the possibility of using *music*, the most abstract of all the arts, for moral or immoral ends is considerably less, even assuming that such a thing as moral or immoral music can exist. The leisurely andante with which a striptease artist undresses in public today may be used tomorrow at the funeral of an accountant of unblemished reputation. 'You may well smile at Wagner's vegetarian proselytizing, but his anti-Semitism cannot be dismissed quite so easily as a negligible quantity,' says Pierre Boulez. Undoubtedly. Fortunately, music is incapable of conveying in sound this sort of primitivism. Indeed, if we were to limit our attentions only to those classical and Romantic composers who were not anti-Semitic, then Orpheus could decently hang up his lyre.

Both Wagner and Wagner's enemies have overestimated the influence of his music. Wagner thought that music—*his* music—would cure the masses of the social evils of the day. Wagner's enemies claim that the Third Reich was built out of the notes of his music. This is a gross misconception. Wagner is not a panacea for the inadequacies of society any more than he can be said to have succeeded as a composer at the time of the totalitarian state in Germany. After all, what use could National Socialism make of *Der Ring des Nibelungen*? There are just two conditions which must be met by any composer working under a totalitarian regime. The first is that his works must not be pessimistic and the second is that they must not be complicated. Measured against these criteria, Wagner was certainly not a totalitarian composer, since his music is anything but optimistic, in addition to which it is inordinately complex.

In the years following the end of the Second World War, society has developed at such an alarming rate that we have the impression of living in a world of unlimited potential. Everything is possible, everything is available, from aspirins to atom bombs. And yet, for all that, we are apparently not yet capable of the most undemanding of intellectual exercises, which is to distinguish art from life. Richard Wagner may have been an unpleasant individual (although I am not entirely convinced of that fact) and his theories were undoubtedly unappetizing. The unpleasant individual is now lying three feet under the ground in the back garden at Wahnfried. And what of the theorist? Immerse yourself in volume seven of Wagner's *Collected Works* while walking along the Nibelungenstrasse in Bayreuth, and even the most fanatical Wagnerian will shake his head. The man and the theorist are dead and buried, by which I do not mean that they are uninteresting as a phenomenon, but rather that for the most part they lie in the shadow of the composer. His megalomania, his womanizing and his silk underwear are, a century, a century-and-a-half after the event, about as artificially relevant as Flaubert's bad breath and Proust's chilblains.

It was bad luck for the composer that our own contemporary, Adolf Hitler, thought he could see in Wagner a kindred spirit. The result of all this was that right up until today responsibility for the Second World War continues to be laid at Wagner's door. But luckily not by everyone. One of the curiosities in my own Wagner library is the three-volume, somewhat romanticized life of Wagner by Zdenko von Kraft. The book itself is not up to much; but the copy in my possession derives its value chiefly from its title-page. From this, it transpires that the book was given as a present on 6 December 1945 to the Jewish officer in charge of the Hotel Eberfeld in Amsterdam, which was being used as a reception centre for prisoners returning home from Theresienstadt. The title-page includes a list of what, for the most part, are good Jewish names such as Hamburger, Weinberg, Engelsman, Goldstein and Leibowitz. They were understanding men who refused to allow their musical tastes to be dictated to by a handful of illiterate Nazis. And they were certainly more understanding than their relatives in modern-day Israel, who threw folding chairs when the Israel Philharmonic Orchestra made an attempt to play the

Prelude to Wagner's *Tristan und Isolde*. Let me say loudly and clearly: they are barbarians, they behave towards Wagner in exactly the same way that the Nazis behaved towards Mendelssohn–they stigmatized a great composer for reasons that have nothing to do with his music.

There is one argument which present-day anti-Wagnerians have frequently overlooked, and that is the *quality* of Wagner's works. In the summer of 1969, the aged conductor Otto Klemperer was interviewed on BBC Radio. He had just recorded the first act of *Die Walküre* with what remained of his failing strength. 'I find it extremely exciting music,' Klemperer said. 'Extremely exciting! You can say a great deal about Wagner but there's nobody who wrote music like it! Nobody!'

These words by a great (and, indeed, Jewish) artist cannot be dismissed lightly. You can become irritated by the edifying tone of *Lohengrin*; you can harbour suspicions about the ideological content of *Parsifal*; you can have ironical reservations about the Teutonic eccentricities of *Die Meistersinger*; and you can question the poetical value of Wagner's libretti ('Hoch über aller Welt ist Gott, und sein Erbarmen ist kein Spott'). But Wagner's music is neither banal nor uninteresting. How many statements by unimpeachable and qualified experts do I have to lay on the table before our present-day anti-Wagnerians are prepared to take account of this fact in their deliberations? It is difficult to discuss the matter seriously with many of Wagner's detractors because their loathing of Wagner the man has prevented them from listening to Wagner the composer. That is why I say to them: believe me, Wagner's music is actually better than it sounds–or it sounds better than it is. I cannot remember who thought up this *aperçu*, nor what the correct version of it is. But both versions are true.

The fact that critical contemporaries who suffered under

his all-embracing personality condemned him for causing scandals and running up debts is all too easy to understand. The same is true of the fact that leftists and liberals alike ceremoniously refused to have anything to do with the artistic tastes of the German Nationalists of the Weimar Republic or the Nazis of the Third Reich. But the war has been over now for nearly forty years and it is time for an end to be put to such nonsense. More than four generations have passed since Wagner hawked around his ideas about Christ as an Aryan and about pure, Germanic blood.

His political tracts, which were already largely out of date by the time they appeared in print, are now gathering mould in second-hand bookshops, while his *Tristan*, *Lohengrin*, *Fliegender Holländer* and *Parsifal* are as alive today as on the day they were born. Wagner created the most up-to-date theatre of the nineteenth century, while *we*, who live in the twentieth century, still sit staring out at each other from over-elaborate boxes in the most old-fashioned *bonbonnières*.

Wagner's ideological falsifiers have been dead and buried for half a century and the few who are still alive are dragged up the Green Hill in their wheel-chairs. Bayreuth really has been denazified–and that is true, implicitly, of Richard Wagner as well, the most famous inhabitant of the parish. Enough is enough. It is time that we finally made our peace with him.

Bibliography and discography

The incalculable number of books on Wagner has grown even bigger in the wake of the hundredth anniversary of the *Ring* in 1976 and the centenary of the composer's death in 1983. As a result, my earlier announcement to the effect that only Jesus Christ and Napoleon Bonaparte have had more written about them may well have been overtaken by events in the meantime. Such a vast amount of secondary material has forced me to be highly selective in preparing the present book. What follows is a broad survey of the principal sources which I have used. It should be regarded partly as a justification and partly (something which is especially true of the discography) as an attempt at consumer guidance.

Wagner's autobiography *Mein Leben* was published in 1963 in an edition by Martin Gregor-Dellin (List Verlag). There exists a facsimile edition of Wagner's complete works (Georg Ohms Verlag) but for my own purposes I have relied upon the 1911 edition of the *Sämtliche Schriften und Dichtungen*, published by Breitkopf & Härtel. There are also a number of fairly recent and on the whole knowledgeably annotated selections from Wagner's collected writings, two of which are worth mentioning. Tibor Kneif (Roger & Bernhard, 1975) has edited the triptych *Die Kunst und die Revolution*, *Das Judenthum in der Musik* and *Was ist deutsch?* A number of articles from the composer's adolescent period form the basis of the collection *Wagner writes from Paris*, translated and edited by Robert L. Jacobs and Geoffrey Skelton (George Allen & Unwin, 1973). Wagner's complete libretti, together with introductions and afterwords, are available in the series Deutscher Taschenbuchverlag (dtv), under the title *Die Musikdramen* (1973).

There are biographies of every shape and size. Typical of the pro-Wagner faction are Ferdinand Pfohl's *Richard Wagner: sein Leben und Schaffen* (Ullstein, 1910) and Curt von Westernhagen's *Wagner* (Atlantis, 1978; English translation by Mary Whittall, Cambridge University Press, 1978). Two of their polemical opponents are Ludwig Marcuse (*Das denkwürdige Leben Richard Wagners*, Munich, 1963) and Robert Gutman, whose book *Richard Wagner, the man, his mind and his music* (Secker & Warburg, 1968) is as vitriolic as it is penetrating. Also worth recommending without further ado are Hans Mayer's *Wagner* (rororo, 1959), Guy de Pourtalès' *Richard Wagner, histoire d'un artiste* (Editions Gallimard, 1932), John Chancellor's *Wagner* (Granada, 1978) and, above all, Martin Gregor-Dellin's *Richard Wagner: sein Leben, sein Werk, sein Jahrhundert* (Piper, 1980).

Other works which I have consulted include: Martin Gregor-Dellin, *Richard Wagner, die Revolution als Oper* (Hanser, 1973); Hans Mayer, *Richard Wagner in Bayreuth* (Suhrkamp, 1978); Bryan Magee, *Aspects of Wagner* (Panther, 1972); Curt von Westernhagen, *Vom Holländer zum Parsifal: neue Wagner-Studien* (Atlantis, 1962); Peter Wapnewski, *Richard Wagner: die Szene und ihr Meister* (C.H. Beck, 1978); Peter Burbidge and Richard Sutton (editors), *The Wagner Companion* (Faber & Faber, 1979); and Hans Mayer, *Anmerkungen zu Richard Wagner* (Suhrkamp, 1977). Thomas Mann's *Wagner und unsere Zeit* (Fischer, 1963) contains practically everything that this particular lover of Wagner ever wrote about the composer, including his famous speech 'Leiden und Grösse Richard Wagners'. Leo

Fremgen's collection of essays, *Richard Wagner heute: Wesen, Werk, Verwirklichung: ein Triptychon* (Heusenstamm: Orion Heimreiter, 1977), also deserves to be mentioned here. The writer considers 'the time not yet ripe' for a public discussion about Wagner's treatise on Judaism in music; on closer investigation it emerges that Fremgen is the musical contributor to the neo-Nazi *Deutsche National-Zeitung*. Two leading essays produced by the Frankfurt School are both published by Suhrkamp. Theodor W. Adorno's *Versuch über Wagner* appeared in a paperback edition in 1974 (English translation, *In Search of Wagner*, by Rodney Livingstone, NLB, 1981); and Ernst Bloch's 'Rettung Wagners durch surrealistische Kolportage' forms part of the collection *Zur Philosophie der Musik* (1974).

Attention may also be drawn to the existence of two series of books on music criticism in which various aspects of Wagner have come under review. The first series is that of *rororo-opernbücher*, which to date have included monographs on *Die Meistersinger von Nürnberg* (1981) and *Der fliegende Holländer* (1982). The second series is that of *Musikkonzepte*, published by edition text + kritik. 1982 saw the publication of a special number devoted to *Parsifal*, which had been preceded in 1978 by an issue with the fascinating title *Richard Wagner: wie antisemitisch darf ein Künstler sein?* ('Richard Wagner: how anti-Semitic is an artist entitled to be?').

The first hundred years of the Bayreuth Festival were recorded in three documentary studies. Herbert Barth's *Richard Wagners Werk in Bayreuth* (dtv, 1976) includes well-known and less well-known classics of Wagnerian literature. Hartmut Zelinsky (*Richard Wagner: ein deutsches Thema*, Zweitausendeins, 1976) has cutting things to say about the human, all too human aspects of Wagner's life and works. Particularly worth while is Michael Karbaum's *Studien zur Geschichte der Bayreuther Festspiele* (Gustav Bosse, 1976).

The author, a historian by profession, gained access to the Wahnfried archives but when he announced his intention of making his findings public, his book was held up for two years by a veto imposed by the Wagner family.

Further details about the musical life of Germany during the period 1933 to 1945 may be found in Józef Wulf's *Musik im Dritten Reich* (Sigbert Mohn Verlag, 1963) and Fred K. Prieberg's *Musik im NS-Staat* (Fischer, 1982). Specially tailored to the Festival town itself is Meta Kropf's nostalgic little book *Bayreuther Festspielsommer von damals*, an account of the long winter of 1936 to 1944 (privately published, 1978).

Books on New Bayreuth include Friedrich Herzfeld's *Das neue Bayreuth* (Rembrandt, 1960) and Geoffrey Skelton's *Wieland Wagner, the positive sceptic* (Victor Gollancz, 1971). An amusing account of a visit to New Bayreuth is contained in Bernard Levin's *Conducted Tour* (Jonathan Cape, 1981), while the no less amusing account of Tchaikovsky's visit to *Old* Bayreuth may be found in Peter Ilych Tchaikovsky, *Erinnerungen und Musikkritiken* (Reclam, 1974; English translation in Robert Hartford, *Bayreuth, the early years*, Victor Gollancz, 1980).

A number of remarks on Heinrich Heine are based on the latter's collected works in the *Säkularausgabe*, published jointly by the Nationale Forschungs- und Gedenkstätten der klassischen deutschen Literatur in Weimar and the Centre national de la recherche scientifique in Paris, 1970ff; the English translation used in the text is by Edgar Alfred Bowring (London, 1872). Anyone writing about Jacques Offenbach will inevitably turn to Siegfried Kracauer's *Jacques Offenbach und das Paris seiner Zeit* (Suhrkamp, 1976). Giacomo Meyerbeer occupies a central position in Heinz Becker's 1980 rororo biography. Zdenko von Kraft has written a book on *Der Sohn* (Siegfried Wagner), published by Stocker in 1980. The best life of Toscanini is that by Harvey Sachs (*Toscanini*, Weidenfeld & Nicolson, 1978). The critical writings of Eduard Hanslick have once more been made available thanks to a photographic reprint of his *Vom musikalischen Schönen* (Breitkopf & Härtel, 1975), and his autobiography, *Aus meinem Leben* (Gregg International Publishers Ltd, 1971). There is also a cheap, but excellent and comprehensive selection from his *Musik-kritiken*, published in 1972 by the East German Reclam-Verlag. For an English translation, the reader is referred to *Vienna's Golden Years of Music 1850–1900*, translated and edited by Henry Pleasants III, Victor Gollancz, 1951. A complete English translation of Nietzsche's writings, by Oscar Levy, appeared in London and New York between 1903 and 1913 and includes the specific polemics against Wagner; it was reprinted by Russell and Russell in 1964. The best-informed life of Nietzsche is the one by Curt Paul Janz (Hanser, 1978), while H.F. Peters has produced a portrait of the philosopher's sister, Elisabeth Nietzsche, entitled *Zarathustra's Sister* (Crown, 1977). Dietrich Fischer-Dieskau has written a thoroughly acceptable account on the subject of *Wagner and Nietzsche* (Deutsche Verlags-Anstalt, 1974; English translation by Joachim Neugroschel, Sidgwick & Jackson, 1978).

Documentation relating to Cosima Wagner is also slowly beginning to assume respectable proportions. The most important publication in this context is of course her Diaries, published in 1976/1977 by Piper Verlag in an edition which shows very few signs of haste on the part of Martin Gregor-Dellin and Dietrich Mack. The English translation is by Geoffrey Skelton (Collins, 1978/1980). This particular document ends in 1883, the year of Wagner's death, but it has found a kind of supplement in the letters and notes of his widow, which appeared in 1980 (also from Piper) under the title *Das zweite Leben*. Her correspondence with Richard Strauss was published in 1978 in an edition by

Franz Trenner and Gabriele Strauss. I have also had the pleasure of quoting from Richard Graf Du Moulin Eckart's biography of the First Lady of the Green Hill (Drei Masken Verlag, 1929/1931), a work which is as voluminous as it is sycophantic.

I shall spare the reader a catalogue of all the biographies, detailed studies, works of criticism, marginalia and curiosities which I have consulted. It will be noted, however, that I have made extensive use of Bayreuth Festival programmes, which every year contain a number of articles of high quality. This book finally owes its existence to my weekly reading of the arts reviews in the weekly newspaper *Die Zeit* and my daily reading of the Bavarian page of the *Süddeutsche Zeitung*.

From a discographical point of view, those listeners who are interested in Wagner might appear to be well catered-for. In practice, however, the results are fairly disappointing. Once again, recordings of Wagner's operas are handicapped by the extremely strenuous demands which the composer makes of his performers. Wagner certainly invented a new musical language, but he unfortunately forgot to devise vocal cords to go with it. In this respect, he has a great deal in common with Ludwig van Beethoven, whose inordinately complex opera *Fidelio* has only rarely, if ever, been adequately recorded.

The following selection is chiefly notable for the glimpse which it affords of my own particular dislike of present-day hi-fi fetishists who are seized by a spontaneous convulsion at the least sign of wow, flutter or rumble. Well, I'm no great lover of wow myself, but I care even less for the fact that intelligent, well-planned opera recordings are becoming increasingly difficult to find in an industry obsessed with the primacy of 'full frequency stereophonic surround sonicstage sound'.

However:

Der fliegende Holländer—There *is* no satisfactory recording of *Der fliegende Holländer*, because of the unique difficulties posed not only by the title-role but also by those of his female counterpart, Senta. The only conductor who, orchestrally at least, achieves commendable results is Otto Klemperer, with the New Philharmonia Orchestra (EMI).

Lohengrin—Fritz Busch in a recording dating from 1947, with the chorus and orchestra of the Metropolitan Opera. The two most important roles are entrusted to the old gold of Helen Traubel and Lauritz Melchior (Cetra).

Tannhäuser—George Szell in a recording dating from 1942, with the chorus and orchestra of the Metropolitan Opera. Once again with Helen Traubel and Lauritz Melchior, supplemented by the bass Alexander Kipnis (Melodram).

Tristan und Isolde—There are two more-or-less contemporary recordings of this opera, both of which leave nothing to be desired. The older of the two, made in 1966, is conducted by Karl Böhm, with the Bayreuth Festival orchestra, and has Birgit Nilsson as Isolde and Wolfgang Windgassen as Tristan. A more recent recording, issued in 1981, is conducted by Reginald Goodall in charge of (*nota bene*) the chorus and orchestra of the Welsh National Opera; Isolde is sung by Linda Esther Gray and Tristan by John Mitchinson. These are two searing interpretations, recorded respectively by DGG and Decca.

Die Meistersinger von Nürnberg—Arturo Toscanini as guest conductor at the 1937 Salzburg Festival is *hors concours*. The orchestra is the Vienna Philharmonic. Toscanini's approach

159

is so fresh, intelligent and unorthodox that the sisters Eva and Daniela sat trembling in their box (Melodram).

Der Ring des Nibelungen–Herbert von Karajan and Pierre Boulez, with two top orchestras at their disposal (the Berlin Philharmonic and that of the Bayreuth Festival, respectively), are of course not lightly dismissed. But my personal preference is for the *Ring* made by Reginald Goodall and the English National Opera, recorded live at the London Coliseum. How is it that Goodall, one of the great Wagner conductors of our day, has never made a name for himself in Europe, let alone in Bayreuth? Unlike his recording of *Tristan und Isolde* listed above, his *Ring* is sung in English, which for a start spares the listener Wagner's frightful alliterative excesses (EMI).

Parsifal–Vittorio Gui in 1950 with the chorus and orchestra of Italian Radio in Rome, sung by some of the world's greatest vocalists: Maria Callas as Kundry, Boris Christoff as Gurnemanz and Rolando Panerai as Amfortas. Rarely has Wagner been so powerfully projected across the footlights: German seriousness tempered by the Mediterranean sun (Foyer).

Three German, three English and two American orchestras, plus one each from Austria and Italy; four German, two English and two Italian conductors, plus one Hungarian and one Frenchman; a good many German–but just as many non-German–Tristans, Fasolts, Isoldes, Fafners, Wotans and Brünnhildes. You can blame my own highly subjective choice for all this, but I would not exclude the possibility that Wagner himself, in his cosmopolitanism, might well have approved.

Index

161

163

admiration for 61–2; Wagner's later condemnation of 62, 70; accused of showmanship 62; suffers anti-Semitic attacks 63; and Offenbach 64–6; and Heine 66; Becker on 154; *L'Africaine* 61; *Les Huguenots* 61, 64, 93, 137; *Robert le diable* 61

Meysenbug, Malwida von 54
Michelangelo Buonarroti 21
Mitchinson, John 159
Mnouchkine, Ariana 92
Mosley, Oswald 131
Mottl, Felix 97–8, 100
Mozart, Wolfgang Amadeus 21, 42, 75, 101, 111, 138, 146–7; *Don Giovanni* 93; *Die Zauberflöte* 26, 74, 106–7, 138, 146
Muck, Karl 105–6, 141
Mussolini, Benito 104, 108

Napoleon Bonaparte 6, 153
Napoleon III 65
Neugroschel, Joachim 157
Neumann, Angelo 59
Newman, Ernest 8
Niebelungensage als Entwurf zu einem Drama, Die 40, 43
Nicolai, Otto 72
Nietzsche, Elisabeth distortion of brother's ideas 7–8, 54; friendship with Cosima 7–8; marriage with Bernhard Förster 10; relationship with brother 53, 56, 72; biography 157
Nietzsche, Friedrich criticism of *Mein Leben* 6; and Elisabeth Nietzsche 7–8, 53, 56, 72; manipulated by National Socialists 8, 119; break with Wagner 7, 11, 20, 49–56; his insanity 25, 53; relationship with Wagner 47–55; and *Tristan* 47; visits to Tribschen and Wahnfried 48–9; vegetarianism 49; Stekel's psycho-sexual study on 51; anti-Germanism of 51; final meeting with Wagner 54–5; and *Parsifal* 54–5; lacking in sense of humour 71–2; as failed musician 116; Lukács on 119;

writings in English 157; biography 157; *Der Fall Wagner* 51–3; *Die Geburt der Tragödie* 19–20; *Nietzsche contra Wagner* 51, 53; *Richard Wagner in Bayreuth* 50

Nilsson, Birgit 159
Not, Die 39

Offenbach, Jacques as Wagner's rival 63–6; and Hanslick 64; satire of Wagner 64–5; Wagner's criticism of 64–5, 84; popularity in Paris 63, 65; Kracauer on 156; *La belle Hélène* 64; *Les contes d'Hoffmann* 72; *La grande duchesse de Gerolstein* 64–5, 137

Oper und Drama 25
Orff, Carl 113
Ossietzky, Carl von 85, 120

Panerai, Rolando 160
Parsifal street in Bayreuth named after 1; Gobineau's alleged influence on 9; conducted by Levi 9, 58, 98; as tract on animal protectionism 15, 34, 114; Prelude performed in Munich 29; incest motif 31; compared to *Ring* 43; zealotry of audiences 45; Nietzsche and 54–5; admired by Weininger 59, 85; influence of Heine 69; different interpretations 84–9, 151; its Christianity 84–5; applause 84–5; pacifism of 85; influence of Schopenhauer 85; and vegetarianism 85; and anti-feminism 85; alleged Aryanism 85–6; alleged anti-Semitism 86–8, 141; as paean to sexual union 87; beauty of score 88; Cosima's desire to have grail scene performed at Wagner's funeral 90–91; flowermaidens 84, 95, 141; and Muck 105, 141; and Toscanini 106; described as boring by Wagner's grandchildren 114; Roller's 1933 production 116–17, 122, 127; Rosenberg on 122;

167

168